MznLnx

Missing Links Exam Preps

Exam Prep for

Discrete Mathematics with Graph Theory

Goodaire & Parmenter, 2nd Edition

The MznLnx Exam Prep is your link from the texbook and lecture to your exams.
The MznLnx Exam Preps are unauthorized and comprehensive reviews of your textbooks.

All material provided by MznLnx and Rico Publications (c) 2010
Textbook publishers and textbook authors do not particpate in or contribute to these reviews.

MznLnx

Rico
Publications

Exam Prep for Discrete Mathematics with Graph Theory
2nd Edition
Goodaire & Parmenter

Publisher: Raymond Houge
Assistant Editor: Michael Rouger
Text and Cover Designer: Lisa Buckner
Marketing Manager: Sara Swagger
Project Manager, Editorial Production: Jerry Emerson
Art Director: Vernon Lowerui

Product Manager: Dave Mason
Editorial Assitant: Rachel Guzmanji
Pedagogy: Debra Long
Cover Image: Jim Reed/Getty Images
Text and Cover Printer: City Printing, Inc.
Compositor: Media Mix, Inc.

(c) 2010 Rico Publications
ALL RIGHTS RESERVED. No part of this work covered by the copyright may be reproduced or used in any form or by an means--graphic, electronic, or mechanical, including photocopying, recording, taping, Web distribution, information storage, and retrieval systems, or in any other manner--without the written permission of the publisher.

For more information about our products, contact us at:
Dave.Mason@RicoPublications.com

For permission to use material from this text or product, submit a request online to:
Dave.Mason@RicoPublications.com

Printed in the United States
ISBN:

Contents

CHAPTER 1
Yes, There are Proofs! — 1

CHAPTER 2
Sets and Relations — 10

CHAPTER 3
Functions — 23

CHAPTER 4
The Integers — 31

CHAPTER 5
Induction and Recursion — 47

CHAPTER 6
Principles of Counting — 56

CHAPTER 7
Permutations and Combinations — 59

CHAPTER 8
Algorithms — 63

CHAPTER 9
Graphs — 73

CHAPTER 10
Paths and Circuits — 78

CHAPTER 11
Applications of Paths and Circuits — 88

CHAPTER 12
Trees — 92

CHAPTER 13
Depth-First Search and Applications — 97

CHAPTER 14
Planar Graphs and Colorings — 100

CHAPTER 15
The Max Flow-Min Cut Theorem — 105

ANSWER KEY — 110

TO THE STUDENT

COMPREHENSIVE

The *MznLnx* Exam Prep series is designed to help you pass your exams. Editors at MznLnx review your textbooks and then prepare these practice exams to help you master the textbook material. Unlike study guides, workbooks, and practice tests provided by the texbook publisher and textbook authors, *MznLnx* gives you **all** of the material in each chapter in exam form, not just samples, so you can be sure to nail your exam.

MECHANICAL

The MznLnx Exam Prep series creates exams that will help you learn the subject matter as well as test you on your understanding. Each question is designed to help you master the concept. Just working through the exams, you gain an understanding of the subject--its a simple mechanical process that produces success.

INTEGRATED STUDY GUIDE AND REVIEW

MznLnx is not just a set of exams designed to test you, its also a comprehensive review of the subject content. Each exam question is also a review of the concept, making sure that you will get the answer correct without having to go to other sources of material. You learn as you go! Its the easiest way to pass an exam.

HUMOR

Studying can be tedious and dry. MznLnx's instructional design includes moderate humor within the exam questions on occassion, to break the tedium and revitalize the brain

Chapter 1. Yes, There are Proofs!

1. In computational complexity theory, the complexity class _____ is a class of problems having two properties:

   - Any given solution to the problem can be verified quickly; the set of problems with this property is called NP.
   - If the problem can be solved quickly, then so can every problem in NP.

   Although any given solution to such a problem can be verified quickly, there is no known efficient way to locate a solution in the first place; indeed, the most notable characteristic of _____ problems is that no fast solution to them is known. That is, the time required to solve the problem using any currently known algorithm increases very quickly as the size of the problem grows. As a result, the time required to solve even moderately large versions of many of these problems easily reaches into the billions or trillions of years, using any amount of computing power available today. As a consequence, determining whether or not it is possible to solve these problems quickly is one of the principal unsolved problems in computer science today.

   a. Subset sum
   b. 3-partition problem
   c. Quadratic assignment problem
   d. NP-complete

2. _____, in logic and fields that rely on it such as mathematics and philosophy, is a biconditional logical connective between statements. In that it is biconditional, the connective can be likened to the standard material conditional ('if') combined with its reverse ('only if'); hence the name. The result is that the truth of either one of the connected statements requires the truth of the other.

   a. If and only if
   b. Enumerative definition
   c. Algebraic logic
   d. Existential graph

3. In propositional logic, contraposition is a logical relationship between two statements of material implication. A proposition Q is materially implicated by a proposition P when the following relationship holds:

   $$(P \rightarrow Q)$$

   In vernacular terms, this states 'If P then Q', or, 'If Socrates is a man then Socrates is human.' In a conditional such as this, P is called the antecedent and Q the consequent. One statement is the _____ of the other just when its antecedent is the negated consequent of the other, and vice-versa.

   a. Control chart
   b. Contour map
   c. Continuous signal
   d. Contrapositive

Chapter 1. Yes, There are Proofs!

4. In logic and mathematics, _____ or not is an operation on logical values, for example, the logical value of a proposition, that sends true to false and false to true. Intuitively, the _____ of a proposition holds exactly when that proposition does not hold. In grammar, nor is an adverb which acts as a coordinating conjunction.
    a. Syntax
    b. Sentence diagram
    c. 1-center problem
    d. Negation

5. In computer science, the _____ is a graph analysis algorithm for finding shortest paths in a weighted, directed graph. A single execution of the algorithm will find the shortest paths between all pairs of vertices. The _____ is an example of dynamic programming.
    a. Depth-limited search
    b. Floyd-Warshall algorithm
    c. Breadth-first search
    d. Topological sorting

6. _____ is an abbreviation of the Latin phrase 'quod erat demonstrandum' which means literally, 'that which was to be demonstrated'. The phrase is written in its abbreviated form at the end of a mathematical proof or philosophical argument, to signify that the last statement deduced was the one to be demonstrated, so the proof is complete.

   The phrase is a translation into Latin of the original Greek ὅ...περ ἔδει δεῖξαι. (hoper edei deixai) which was used by many early mathematicians including Euclid and Archimedes.

    a. Direct proof
    b. Proofs from THE BOOK
    c. Nonconstructive proof
    d. Q.E.D.

7. In mathematics, computing, linguistics and related subjects, an _____ is a sequence of finite instructions, often used for calculation and data processing. It is formally a type of effective method in which a list of well-defined instructions for completing a task will, when given an initial state, proceed through a well-defined series of successive states, eventually terminating in an end-state. The transition from one state to the next is not necessarily deterministic; some _____s, known as probabilistic _____s, incorporate randomness.
    a. Out-of-core
    b. Approximate counting algorithm
    c. In-place algorithm
    d. Algorithm

Chapter 1. Yes, There are Proofs!

8. In propositional logic, a set of Boolean operators is called _____ if it permits the realisation of any possible truth table.

Using a complete Boolean algebra which does not include XOR (such as the well-known AND OR NOT set), this function can be realised as follows:

(a or b) and not (a and b.)

However, other complete Boolean algebras are possible, such as NAND or NOR (either gate can form a complete Boolean algebra by itself - the proof is detailed on their pages.)

   a. Logical biconditional
   b. First-order predicate calculus
   c. Counterfactual conditional
   d. Sufficient

9. In logic, the words necessity and sufficiency refer to the implicational relationships between statements. The assertion that one statement is a _____ condition of another means that the former statement is true if and only if the latter is true.

   - A necessary condition of a statement must be satisfied for the statement to be true. Formally, a statement P is a necessary condition of a statement Q if Q implies P. For example, the ability to breathe is necessary to a human's survival. Likewise, for the whole numbers greater than two, being odd is necessary to being prime, since two is the only whole number that is both even and prime.

   - A sufficient condition is one that, if satisfied, assures the statement's truth. Formally, a statement P is a sufficient condition of a statement Q if P implies Q. Thus, jumping is sufficient to leave the ground, since an intrinsic element of the concept jumping is leaving the ground.

   a. Cyclic negation
   b. Monadic predicate calculus
   c. Necessary and sufficient
   d. Logical implication

10. In the study of metric spaces in mathematics, there are various notions of two metrics on the same underlying space being 'the same', or _____.

In the following, M will denote a non-empty set and d_1 and d_2 will denote two metrics on M.

The two metrics d_1 and d_2 are said to be topologically _____ if they generate the same topology on M.

a. Equivalent
b. A Mathematical Theory of Communication
c. A posteriori
d. A chemical equation

11. In mathematics, the _____ is a direct product of sets. The _____ is named after René Descartes, whose formulation of analytic geometry gave rise to this concept.

Specifically, the _____ of two sets X and Y, denoted X × Y, is the set of all possible ordered pairs whose first component is a member of X and whose second component is a member of Y:

$$X \times Y = \{(x, y) | x \in X \text{ and } y \in Y\}.$$

For example, the _____ of the 13-element set of standard playing card ranks {Ace, King, Queen, Jack, 10, 9, 8, 7, 6, 5, 4, 3, 2} and the four-element set of card suits {â™ , â™¥, â™¦, â™£} is the 52-element set of all possible playing cards ,, ...,,, ...,}.

a. Cartesian product
b. Disjoint sets
c. Set of all sets
d. Choice function

12. In mathematics, a _____ is a convincing demonstration that some mathematical statement is necessarily true. _____s are obtained from deductive reasoning, rather than from inductive or empirical arguments. That is, a _____ must demonstrate that a statement is true in all cases, without a single exception.
a. Conchoid
b. Proof
c. Germ
d. Congruent

13. The '_____' puzzle consists of four cubes with faces colored with four colors. The object of the puzzle is to stack these cubes in a column so that each side of the stack shows each of the four colors. The distribution of colors on each cube is unique.
a. Instant Insanity
b. Induced path
c. Eulerian path
d. Independent set

Chapter 1. Yes, There are Proofs! 5

14. In mathematics, a _____ of an integer n is an integer which evenly divides n without leaving a remainder.

For example, 7 is a _____ of 42 because 42/7 = 6. We also say 42 is divisible by 7 or 42 is a multiple of 7 or 7 divides 42 or 7 is a factor of 42 and we usually write 7 | 42.

   a. 2-3 heap
   b. Divisor
   c. 1-center problem
   d. 120-cell

15. In mathematics, the _____, sometimes known as the greatest common factor or highest common factor, of two non-zero integers, is the largest positive integer that divides both numbers without remainder.

This notion can be extended to polynomials, see _____ of two polynomials.

The _____ of a and b is written as gc, or sometimes simply as.

   a. Greatest common divisor
   b. Minuend
   c. Multiplication
   d. Highest common factor

16. In mathematics, a _____ is a number which can be expressed as a ratio of two integers. Non-integer _____s are usually written as the vulgar fraction $\frac{a}{b}$, where b is not zero. a is called the numerator, and b the denominator.
   a. Tally marks
   b. Pre-algebra
   c. Minkowski distance
   d. Rational number

17. A _____ is a mathematical table used in logic -- specifically in connection with Boolean algebra, boolean functions, and propositional calculus -- to compute the functional values of logical expressions on each of their functional arguments, that is, on each combination of values taken by their logical variables. In particular, _____s can be used to tell whether a propositional expression is true for all legitimate input values, that is, logically valid.

The pattern of reasoning that the _____ tabulates was Frege's, Peirce's, and Schröder's by 1880.

a. 120-cell
b. 1-center problem
c. 2-3 heap
d. Truth table

18. _____ is a method of mathematical proof typically used to establish that a given statement is true of all natural numbers. It is done by proving that the first statement in the infinite sequence of statements is true, and then proving that if any one statement in the infinite sequence of statements is true, then so is the next one.

The method can be extended to prove statements about more general well-founded structures, such as trees; this generalization, known as structural induction, is used in mathematical logic and computer science.

a. Mathematical Induction
b. Ground expression
c. Herbrand structure
d. Finitary

19. In mathematics, _____ is a property that a binary operation can have. It means that, within an expression containing two or more of the same associative operators in a row, the order that the operations are performed does not matter as long as the sequence of the operands is not changed. That is, rearranging the parentheses in such an expression will not change its value.
a. Idempotence
b. Associativity
c. Unital
d. Algebraically closed

20. In mathematics, _____ is the ability to change the order of something without changing the end result. It is a fundamental property of many operations throughout mathematics, and many proofs depend on it. The _____ of simple operations, such as multiplication or addition of numbers, was for many years implicitly assumed and the property was not given a name or attributed until the 19th century when mathematicians began to formalize the theory of mathematics.
a. Power set
b. Commutativity
c. Self-adjoint
d. Left alternative

21. _____ describes the property of operations in mathematics and computer science which means that multiple applications of the operation does not change the result. The concept of _____ arises in a number of places in abstract algebra.

There are several meanings of _____, depending on what the concept is applied to:

- A unary operation is called idempotent if, whenever it is applied twice to any value, it gives the same result as if it were applied once. For example, the absolute value function is idempotent as a function from the set of real numbers to the set of real numbers: ab = ab.
- A binary operation is called idempotent if, whenever it is applied to two equal values, it gives that value as the result. For example, the operation giving the maximum value of two values is idempotent: ma = x.
- Given a binary operation, an idempotent element for the operation is a value for which the operation, when given that value for both of its operands, gives the value as the result. For example, the number 1 is an idempotent of multiplication: 1 × 1 = 1.

A unary operation f that is a map from some set S into itself is called idempotent if, for all x in S,

   f

In particular, the identity function id_S, defined by
id_S, is idempotent, as is the constant function K_c, where c is an element of S, defined by $K_c(x) = c$.

   a. Ordered exponential
   b. Idempotence
   c. Antiisomorphism
   d. Absorption law

22. In logic and philosophy, _____ refers to either (a) the 'content' or 'meaning' of a meaningful declarative sentence or (b) the pattern of symbols, marks, or sounds that make up a meaningful declarative sentence. _____s in either case are intended to be truth-bearers, that is, they are either true or false.

The existence of _____s in the former sense, as well as the existence of 'meanings', is disputed.

   a. Logicism
   b. Laws of classical logic
   c. Linear logic
   d. Proposition

23. In boolean logic, a _____ is a standardization of a logical formula which is a disjunction of conjunctive clauses. As a normal form, it is useful in automated theorem proving. A logical formula is considered to be in DNF if and only if it is a disjunction of one or more conjunctions of one or more literals.

a. Prenex normal form
b. Skolem normal form
c. 1-center problem
d. Disjunctive normal form

24. In mathematics, specifically in combinatorial commutative algebra, a convex lattice polytope P is called _____ if it has the following property: given any positive integer n, every lattice point of the dilation nP, obtained from P by scaling its vertices by the factor n and taking the convex hull of the resulting points, can be written as the sum of exactly n lattice points in P. This property plays an important role in the theory of toric varieties, where it corresponds to projective normality of the toric variety determined by P.

The simplex in R^k with the vertices at the origin and along the unit coordinate vectors is _____.

a. Hypercube
b. Normal
c. Polytetrahedron
d. Demihypercubes

25. In game theory, _____ is a way of describing a game. Unlike extensive form, normal-form representations are not graphical per se, but rather represent the game by way of a matrix. While this approach can be of greater use in identifying strictly dominated strategies and Nash equilibria, some information is lost as compared to extensive-form representations.

a. Normal form
b. Word problem
c. Secant
d. Japanese theorem

26. In geometry, a _____ is a convex regular polyhedron. These are the three-dimensional analogs of the convex regular polygons. There are precisely five such figures.

a. 120-cell
b. 1-center problem
c. Platonic solid
d. 2-3 heap

27. _____ is the act or process of deriving a conclusion based solely on what one knows.

_____ is studied within several different fields.

- Human _____ is traditionally studied within the field of cognitive psychology.
- Logic studies the laws of valid _____.
- Statisticians have developed formal rules for _____ from quantitative data.
- Artificial intelligence researchers develop automated _____ systems.

The process by which a conclusion is inferred from multiple observations is called inductive reasoning. The conclusion may be correct or incorrect, or partially correct, or correct to within a certain degree of accuracy, or correct in certain situations.

a. A posteriori
b. A chemical equation
c. A Mathematical Theory of Communication
d. Inference

28. In mathematics, a _____ is a statement that can be proved on the basis of explicitly stated or previously agreed assumptions.
a. Boolean function
b. Logical value
c. Disjunction introduction
d. Theorem

29. In mathematical logic and automated theorem proving, _____ is a rule of inference leading to a refutation theorem-proving technique for sentences in propositional logic and first-order logic. In other words, iteratively applying the _____ rule in a suitable way allows for telling whether a propositional formula is satisfiable and for proving that a first-order formula is unsatisfiable; this method may prove the satisfiability of a first-order satisfiable formula, but not always, as it is the case for all methods for first-order logic. _____ was introduced by John Alan Robinson in 1965.
a. Resolution
b. Foci
c. Free
d. Concurrent

Chapter 2. Sets and Relations

1. In mathematics, a _____ can mean either an element of the set {1, 2, 3, ...} or an element of the set {0, 1, 2, 3, ...}. The latter is especially preferred in mathematical logic, set theory, and computer science.

   _____s have two main purposes: they can be used for counting, and they can be used for ordering.

   a. Suslin cardinal
   b. Strong partition cardinal
   c. Cardinal numbers
   d. Natural number

2. In mathematics, a _____ is a number which can be expressed as a ratio of two integers. Non-integer _____s are usually written as the vulgar fraction $\frac{a}{b}$, where b is not zero. a is called the numerator, and b the denominator.
   a. Rational number
   b. Pre-algebra
   c. Minkowski distance
   d. Tally marks

3. The '_____' puzzle consists of four cubes with faces colored with four colors. The object of the puzzle is to stack these cubes in a column so that each side of the stack shows each of the four colors. The distribution of colors on each cube is unique.
   a. Eulerian path
   b. Instant Insanity
   c. Independent set
   d. Induced path

4. In mathematics, the _____s are an extension of the real numbers obtained by adjoining an imaginary unit, denoted i, which satisfies:

   $$i^2 = -1.$$

   Every _____ can be written in the form a + bi, where a and b are real numbers called the real part and the imaginary part of the _____, respectively.

   _____s are a field, and thus have addition, subtraction, multiplication, and division operations. These operations extend the corresponding operations on real numbers, although with a number of additional elegant and useful properties, e.g., negative real numbers can be obtained by squaring _____s.

a. 120-cell
b. Real part
c. 1-center problem
d. Complex number

5. In mathematics, and more specifically set theory, the _____ is the unique set having no members. Some axiomatic set theories assure that the _____ exists by including an axiom of _____; in other theories, its existence can be deduced. Many possible properties of sets are trivially true for the _____.
   a. Empty function
   b. Inverse function
   c. Empty set
   d. A Mathematical Theory of Communication

6. _____ is a method of mathematical proof typically used to establish that a given statement is true of all natural numbers. It is done by proving that the first statement in the infinite sequence of statements is true, and then proving that if any one statement in the infinite sequence of statements is true, then so is the next one.

The method can be extended to prove statements about more general well-founded structures, such as trees; this generalization, known as structural induction, is used in mathematical logic and computer science.

   a. Ground expression
   b. Herbrand structure
   c. Finitary
   d. Mathematical Induction

7. In mathematics, a _____ is a convincing demonstration that some mathematical statement is necessarily true. _____s are obtained from deductive reasoning, rather than from inductive or empirical arguments. That is, a _____ must demonstrate that a statement is true in all cases, without a single exception.
   a. Germ
   b. Congruent
   c. Conchoid
   d. Proof

8. In mathematics, especially in set theory, a set A is a _____ of a set B if A is 'contained' inside B. Notice that A and B may coincide. The relationship of one set being a _____ of another is called inclusion.

a. Subset
b. Set of all sets
c. Horizontal line test
d. Cartesian product

9. In geometry, a _____ is a convex regular polyhedron. These are the three-dimensional analogs of the convex regular polygons. There are precisely five such figures.
   a. 120-cell
   b. 1-center problem
   c. 2-3 heap
   d. Platonic solid

10. In mathematics, given a set S, the _____ of S, written $\mathcal{P}(S)$, PS, is the set of all subsets of S. In axiomatic set theory, the existence of the _____ of any set is postulated by the axiom of _____.

Any subset F of $\mathcal{P}(S)$ is called a family of sets over S.

   a. Polarization
   b. Power set
   c. Formal derivative
   d. Formal power series

11. _____ or set diagrams are diagrams that show all hypothetically possible logical relations between a finite collection of sets. _____ were invented around 1880 by John Venn. They are used in many fields, including set theory, probability, logic, statistics, and computer science.
   a. 2-3 heap
   b. 1-center problem
   c. 120-cell
   d. Venn diagrams

12. In mathematics, _____ is a property that a binary operation can have. It means that, within an expression containing two or more of the same associative operators in a row, the order that the operations are performed does not matter as long as the sequence of the operands is not changed. That is, rearranging the parentheses in such an expression will not change its value.

a. Algebraically closed
b. Associativity
c. Unital
d. Idempotence

13. A _____ is a 2D geometric symbolic representation of information according to some visualization technique. Sometimes, the technique uses a 3D visualization which is then projected onto the 2D surface. The word graph is sometimes used as a synonym for _____.

   a. 2-3 heap
   b. Diagram
   c. 1-center problem
   d. 120-cell

14. In mathematics, the _____ of two sets A and B is the set that contains all elements of A that also belong to B, but no other elements.

For explanation of the symbols used in this article, refer to the table of mathematical symbols.

The _____ of A and B

The _____ of A and B is written 'A ∩ B'. Formally:

  x is an element of A ∩ B if and only if
  - x is an element of A and
  - x is an element of B.

  For example:
  - The _____ of the sets {1, 2, 3} and {2, 3, 4} is {2, 3}.
  - The number 9 is not in the _____ of the set of prime numbers {2, 3, 5, 7, 11, …} and the set of odd numbers {1, 3, 5, 7, 9, 11, …}.

If the _____ of two sets A and B is empty, that is they have no elements in common, then they are said to be disjoint, denoted: A ∩ B = ∅. For example the sets {1, 2} and {3, 4} are disjoint, written {1, 2} ∩ {3, 4} = ∅.

   a. Intersection
   b. Order
   c. Advice
   d. Erlang

Chapter 2. Sets and Relations

15. In set theory, the term _____ refers to a set operation used in the convergence of set elements to form a resultant set containing the elements of both sets. As a simple example, a _____ of two disjoint sets, which do not have elements in common results in a set containing all elements from both sets. A Venn diagram representing the _____ of sets A and B.
    a. UES
    b. Event
    c. Introduction
    d. Union

16. In mathematics, the _____ is a direct product of sets. The _____ is named after René Descartes, whose formulation of analytic geometry gave rise to this concept.

Specifically, the _____ of two sets X and Y, denoted X × Y, is the set of all possible ordered pairs whose first component is a member of X and whose second component is a member of Y:

$$X \times Y = \{(x, y) | x \in X \text{ and } y \in Y\}.$$

For example, the _____ of the 13-element set of standard playing card ranks {Ace, King, Queen, Jack, 10, 9, 8, 7, 6, 5, 4, 3, 2} and the four-element set of card suits {♠, ♥, ♦, ♣} is the 52-element set of all possible playing cards ,, ...,, ...,}.

   a. Cartesian product
   b. Disjoint sets
   c. Choice function
   d. Set of all sets

17. In discrete mathematics and predominantly in set theory, a _____ is a concept used in comparisons of sets to refer to the unique values of one set in relation to another. The terms 'absolute' and 'relative' _____ refer to more specific applications of the concept, with universal _____s referring to elements unique to the universal set and the latter referring to the unique elements of one set in relation to another. In this image, the universal set is represented by the border of the image, and the set A as a disc.
    a. Kernel
    b. Complement
    c. Derivative algebra
    d. Huge

Chapter 2. Sets and Relations

18. In combinatorics, a (v,k,λ) _____ is a subset D of a group G such that the order of G is v, the size of D is k, and every nonidentity element of G can be expressed as a product $d_1 d_2^{-1}$ of elements of D in exactly λ ways.

- A simple counting argument shows that there are exactly $k^2 - k$ pairs of elements from D that will yield nonidentity elements, so every _____ must satisfy the equation $k^2 - k = (v - 1)\lambda$.
- If D is a _____, and $g \in G$, then $gD = \{gd : d \in D\}$ is also a _____, and is called a translate of D.
- The set of all translates of a _____ D forms a symmetric design (a special kind of combinatorial design.) In such a design there are v elements (mostly called points) and v blocks. Each block of the design consists of k points, each point is contained in k blocks. Any two blocks have exactly λ elements in common and any two points are 'joined' by λ blocks. The group G then acts as an automorphism group of the design. It is sharply transitive on points and blocks.
- Since every _____ gives a combinatorial design, the parameter set must satisfy the Bruck-Chowla-Ryser theorem.
- Not every combinatorial design gives a _____.

In particular, if λ = 1, then the _____ gives rise to a projective plane. An example of a (7,3,1) _____ in the group $\mathbb{Z}/7\mathbb{Z}$ is the set {1,2,4}. The translates of this _____ gives the Fano plane.

a. Transversal
b. Macdonald polynomials
c. Combinatorial class
d. Difference set

19. In computational complexity theory, the complexity class _____ is a class of problems having two properties:

- Any given solution to the problem can be verified quickly; the set of problems with this property is called NP.
- If the problem can be solved quickly, then so can every problem in NP.

Although any given solution to such a problem can be verified quickly, there is no known efficient way to locate a solution in the first place; indeed, the most notable characteristic of _____ problems is that no fast solution to them is known. That is, the time required to solve the problem using any currently known algorithm increases very quickly as the size of the problem grows. As a result, the time required to solve even moderately large versions of many of these problems easily reaches into the billions or trillions of years, using any amount of computing power available today. As a consequence, determining whether or not it is possible to solve these problems quickly is one of the principal unsolved problems in computer science today.

a. Subset sum
b. Quadratic assignment problem
c. 3-partition problem
d. NP-complete

Chapter 2. Sets and Relations

20. In mathematics, a _____ is a statement that can be proved on the basis of explicitly stated or previously agreed assumptions.
    a. Theorem
    b. Boolean function
    c. Disjunction introduction
    d. Logical value

21. In mathematics, a _____ is a set of real numbers with the property that any number that lies between two numbers in the set is also included in the set. For example, the set of all numbers x satisfying $0 \leq x \leq 1$ is an _____ which contains 0 and 1, as well as all numbers between them. Other examples of _____s are the set of all real numbers $\mathbb{R}$, the set of all positive real numbers, and the empty set.
    a. Annihilator
    b. Ideal
    c. Order
    d. Interval

22. _____ IPA: [pjɛːʁ ɛ dəˈfɛːʁ 'ma] (17 August 1601 or 1607/8 - 12 January 1665) was a French lawyer at the Parlement of Toulouse, France, and a mathematician who is given credit for early developments that led to modern calculus. In particular, he is recognized for his discovery of an original method of finding the greatest and the smallest ordinates of curved lines, which is analogous to that of the then unknown differential calculus, as well as his research into the theory of numbers. He also made notable contributions to analytic geometry, probability, and optics.
    a. Pierre de Fermat
    b. Nikita Borisov
    c. Felix Hausdorff
    d. Philip J. Davis

23. In mathematics, one can often define a _____ of objects already known, giving a new one. This is generally the Cartesian product of the underlying sets, together with a suitably defined structure on the product set. More abstractly, one talks about the product in category theory, which formalizes these notions.
    a. Power set
    b. Linear combinations
    c. Closure with a twist
    d. Direct product

24. In quantum field theory and statistical mechanics in the thermodynamic limit, a system with a global symmetry can have more than one phase. For parameters where the symmetry is spontaneously broken, the system is said to be _____. When the global symmetry is unbroken the system is disordered.

a. Isoenthalpic-isobaric ensemble
b. Ordered
c. Einstein relation
d. Ursell function

25. In mathematics, an _____ is a collection of objects having two coordinates (or entries or projections), such that one can always uniquely determine the object, which is the first coordinate (or first entry or left projection) of the pair as well as the second coordinate (or second entry or right projection.) If the first coordinate is a and the second is b, the usual notation for an _____ is (a, b.) The pair is 'ordered' in that (a, b) differs from (b, a) unless a = b.
a. A Mathematical Theory of Communication
b. A chemical equation
c. Ordered pair
d. A posteriori

26. In functional analysis, a Banach space is called _____ if it satisfies a certain abstract property involving dual spaces. _____ spaces turn out to have desirable geometric properties.

Suppose X is a normed vector space over R or C.

a. Boolean algebra
b. Copula
c. Reflexive
d. Gamma test

27. In mathematics, a binary relation R on a set X is _____ if, for all a and b in X, if a is R to b and b is R to a, then a = b.

In mathematical notation, this is:

$$\forall a, b \in X, \; aRb \wedge bRa \; \Rightarrow \; a = b$$

or equally,

$$\forall a, b \in X, \; aRb \wedge a \neq b \Rightarrow \neg bRa.$$

Inequalities are _____, since for numbers a and b, a ≤ b and b ≤ a if and only if a = b. The same holds for subsets.

a. Erlang
b. ISAAC
c. Association
d. Antisymmetric

28. _____ is an abbreviation of the Latin phrase 'quod erat demonstrandum' which means literally, 'that which was to be demonstrated'. The phrase is written in its abbreviated form at the end of a mathematical proof or philosophical argument, to signify that the last statement deduced was the one to be demonstrated, so the proof is complete.

The phrase is a translation into Latin of the original Greek ἅ½...περ ἅ¼"δει δειξαι. (hoper edei deixai) which was used by many early mathematicians including Euclid and Archimedes.

a. Nonconstructive proof
b. Proofs from THE BOOK
c. Direct proof
d. Q.E.D.

29. In set theory and its applications throughout mathematics, a _____ is a collection of sets that can be unambiguously defined by a property that all its members share. The precise definition of '_____' depends on foundational context. In work on ZF set theory, the notion of _____ is informal, whereas other set theories, such as NBG set theory, axiomatize the notion of '_____'.
a. Coherence
b. Filter
c. Congruent
d. Class

30. In mathematics, given a set X and an equivalence relation ~ on X, the _____ of an element a in X is the subset of all elements in X which are equivalent to a:

$$[a] = \{x \in X | x \sim a\}.$$

The notion of _____es is useful for constructing sets out of already constructed ones. The set of all _____es in X given an equivalence relation ~ is usually denoted as X / ~ and called the quotient set of X by ~. This operation can be thought of as the act of 'dividing' the input set by the equivalence relation, hence both the name 'quotient', and the notation, which are both reminiscent of division.

a. Equivalence class
b. A chemical equation
c. Equivalence relation
d. A Mathematical Theory of Communication

31. _____, in logic and fields that rely on it such as mathematics and philosophy, is a biconditional logical connective between statements. In that it is biconditional, the connective can be likened to the standard material conditional ('if') combined with its reverse ('only if'); hence the name. The result is that the truth of either one of the connected statements requires the truth of the other.
   a. Algebraic logic
   b. If and only if
   c. Existential graph
   d. Enumerative definition

32. In number theory, a _____ of a positive integer n is a way of writing n as a sum of positive integers. Two sums which only differ in the order of their summands are considered to be the same _____; if order matters then the sum becomes a composition. A summand in a _____ is also called a part.
   a. Partition
   b. Distribution
   c. Derivative algebra
   d. Congruent

33. In mathematics, an _____ in the sense of ring theory is a subring $\mathcal{O}$ of a ring R that satisfies the conditions

   1. R is a ring which is a finite-dimensional algebra over the rational number field $\mathbb{Q}$
   2. $\mathcal{O}$ spans R over $\mathbb{Q}$, so that $\mathbb{Q}\mathcal{O} = R$, and
   3. $\mathcal{O}$ is a lattice in R.

The third condition can be stated more accurately, in terms of the extension of scalars of R to the real numbers, embedding R in a real vector space. In less formal terms, additively $\mathcal{O}$ should be a free abelian group generated by a basis for R over $\mathbb{Q}$.

The leading example is the case where R is a number field K and $\mathcal{O}$ is its ring of integers. In algebraic number theory there are examples for any K other than the rational field of proper subrings of the ring of integers that are also _____s.

a. Efficiency
b. Algebraic
c. Annihilator
d. Order

34. In mathematics, especially order theory, a _____ formalizes the intuitive concept of an ordering, sequencing, or arrangement of the elements of a set. A poset consists of a set together with a binary relation that describes, for certain pairs of elements in the set, the requirement that one of the elements must precede the other. However, a _____ differs from a total order in that some pairs of elements may not be related to each other in this way.
   a. Scott topology
   b. Dedekind cut
   c. Covering relation
   d. Partially ordered set

35. In mathematics, especially order theory, a partially ordered set formalizes the intuitive concept of an ordering, sequencing, or arrangement of the elements of a set. A _____ consists of a set together with a binary relation that describes, for certain pairs of elements in the set, the requirement that one of the elements must precede the other. However, a partially ordered set differs from a total order in that some pairs of elements may not be related to each other in this way.
   a. Poset
   b. Completeness properties
   c. Complete Heyting algebra
   d. Greatest lower bound

36. In mathematics and set theory, a _____, linear order, simple order, or
   a. Well-founded relation
   b. Well-order
   c. Transitive relation
   d. Total order

37. In mathematics, a _____ of a set X is a collection of sets such that X is a subset of the union of sets in the collection. In symbols, if

$$C = \{U_\alpha : \alpha \in A\}$$

is an indexed family of sets U_α, then C is a _____ of X if

$$X \subseteq \bigcup_{\alpha \in A} U_\alpha$$

_____s are commonly used in the context of topology. If the set X is a topological space, then a _____ C of X is a collection of subsets U_α of X whose union is the whole space X.

a. Generalised metric
b. Contractible space
c. Manifold
d. Cover

38. In mathematics, especially in order theory, an upper bound of a subset S of some partially ordered set is an element of P which is greater than or equal to every element of S. The term _____ is defined dually as an element of P which is lesser than or equal to every element of S. A set with an upper bound is said to be bounded from above by that bound, a set with a _____ is said to be bounded from below by that bound.
a. Lower bound
b. Cofinality
c. Partially ordered set
d. Monomial order

39. In mathematics, especially in order theory, an _____ of a subset S of some partially ordered set is an element of P which is greater than or equal to every element of S. The term lower bound is defined dually as an element of P which is lesser than or equal to every element of S. A set with an _____ is said to be bounded from above by that bound, a set with a lower bound is said to be bounded from below by that bound.
a. Order-embedding
b. Upper bound
c. Infinite descending chain
d. Order isomorphism

40. In mathematics, especially in geometry and group theory, a _____ in R^n is a discrete subgroup of R^n which spans the real vector space R^n. Every _____ in R^n can be generated from a basis for the vector space by forming all linear combinations with integral coefficients. A _____ may be viewed as a regular tiling of a space by a primitive cell.

a. Group
b. Lattice
c. Boundary
d. Homogeneity

Chapter 3. Functions

1. An _____ is an artifact, usually two-dimensional (a picture), that has a similar appearance to some subject--usually a physical object or a person.

_____s may be two-dimensional, such as a photograph, screen display, and as well as a three-dimensional, such as a statue. They may be captured by optical devices--such as cameras, mirrors, lenses, telescopes, microscopes, etc.

   a. A Mathematical Theory of Communication
   b. A chemical equation
   c. A posteriori
   d. Image

2. In computational complexity theory, the complexity class _____ is a class of problems having two properties:

   - Any given solution to the problem can be verified quickly; the set of problems with this property is called NP.
   - If the problem can be solved quickly, then so can every problem in NP.

Although any given solution to such a problem can be verified quickly, there is no known efficient way to locate a solution in the first place; indeed, the most notable characteristic of _____ problems is that no fast solution to them is known. That is, the time required to solve the problem using any currently known algorithm increases very quickly as the size of the problem grows. As a result, the time required to solve even moderately large versions of many of these problems easily reaches into the billions or trillions of years, using any amount of computing power available today. As a consequence, determining whether or not it is possible to solve these problems quickly is one of the principal unsolved problems in computer science today.

   a. Quadratic assignment problem
   b. 3-partition problem
   c. NP-complete
   d. Subset sum

3. In propositional logic, contraposition is a logical relationship between two statements of material implication. A proposition Q is materially implied by a proposition P when the following relationship holds:

$$(P \to Q)$$

In vernacular terms, this states 'If P then Q', or, 'If Socrates is a man then Socrates is human.' In a conditional such as this, P is called the antecedent and Q the consequent. One statement is the _____ of the other just when its antecedent is the negated consequent of the other, and vice-versa.

Chapter 3. Functions

   a. Continuous signal
   b. Control chart
   c. Contrapositive
   d. Contour map

4. In mathematics, especially in the area of abstract algebra known as ring theory, a _____ is a ring with 0 ≠ 1 such that ab = 0 implies that either a = 0 or b = 0. That is, it is a nontrivial ring without left or right zero divisors. A commutative _____ is called an integral _____.

   a. Left primitive ring
   b. Modular representation theory
   c. Simple ring
   d. Domain

5. In mathematics, an _____ is a function which associates distinct arguments with distinct values.

An _____ is called an injection, and is also said to be an information-preserving or one-to-one function.

A function f that is not injective is sometimes called many-to-one.

   a. Injective function
   b. A chemical equation
   c. Unary function
   d. A Mathematical Theory of Communication

6. In mathematics, a function f is said to be surjective or _____, if its values span its whole codomain; that is, for every y in the codomain, there is at least one x in the domain such that f(x) = y.

Said another way, a function f: X → Y is surjective if and only if its range f(X) is equal to its codomain Y. A surjective function is called a surjection.

   a. A posteriori
   b. A chemical equation
   c. A Mathematical Theory of Communication
   d. Onto

7. In descriptive statistics, the _____ is the length of the smallest interval which contains all the data. It is calculated by subtracting the smallest observations from the greatest and provides an indication of statistical dispersion.

It is measured in the same units as the data.

a. Bandwidth
b. Range
c. Class
d. Kernel

8. In mathematics, a function f is said to be _____ or onto, if its values span its whole codomain; that is, for every y in the codomain, there is at least one x in the domain such that f

Said another way, a function f: X → Y is _____ if and only if its range f

a. Rotation of axes
b. Linear map
c. High-dimensional model representation
d. Surjective

9. In mathematics, a _____ is a statement that can be proved on the basis of explicitly stated or previously agreed assumptions.
a. Disjunction introduction
b. Boolean function
c. Logical value
d. Theorem

10. In mathematics, the _____ of a real number is its numerical value without regard to its sign. So, for example, 3 is the _____ of both 3 and −3.

The _____ of a number a is denoted by | a |.

Generalizations of the _____ for real numbers occur in a wide variety of mathematical settings.

a. Area hyperbolic functions
b. A Mathematical Theory of Communication
c. A chemical equation
d. Absolute value

11. In mathematics and computer science, the _____ and ceiling functions map real numbers to the next lower and next higher integers.

The _____ function of a real number x, sometimes called the greatest integer or entier function, and denoted variously by [x] $\lfloor x \rfloor$, _____(x), or int(x), is a function whose value is the largest integer less than or equal to x. Formally, for all real numbers x,

$$\lfloor x \rfloor = \max\{n \in \mathbb{Z} \mid n \leq x\}.$$

For example, _____(2.9) = 2, _____(−2) = −2 and _____(−12/5) = −3.

a. 1-center problem
b. 2-3 heap
c. 120-cell
d. Floor

12. The mathematical concept of a _____ expresses the intuitive idea of deterministic dependence between two quantities, one of which is viewed as primary and the other as secondary. A _____ then is a way to associate a unique output for each input of a specified type, for example, a real number or an element of a given set.

a. Going up
b. Function
c. Coherent
d. Grill

13. In mathematics, the term _____ has several different important meanings:

- An _____ is an equality that remains true regardless of the values of any variables that appear within it, to distinguish it from an equality which is true under more particular conditions. For this, the 'triple bar' symbol ≡ is sometimes used.
- In algebra, an _____ or _____ element of a set S with a binary operation · is an element e that, when combined with any element x of S, produces that same x. That is, e·x = x·e = x for all x in S.
    - The _____ function from a set S to itself, often denoted id or id$_S$, s the function such that i = x for all x in S. This function serves as the _____ element in the set of all functions from S to itself with respect to function composition.
    - In linear algebra, the _____ matrix of size n is the n-by-n square matrix with ones on the main diagonal and zeros elsewhere. This matrix serves as the _____ with respect to matrix multiplication.

A common example of the first meaning is the trigonometric _____

$$\sin^2 \theta + \cos^2 \theta = 1$$

which is true for all real values of θ, as opposed to

$$\cos\theta = 1,$$

which is true only for some values of θ, not all. For example, the latter equation is true when $\theta = 0$, false when $\theta = 2$

The concepts of 'additive _____' and 'multiplicative _____' are central to the Peano axioms. The number 0 is the 'additive _____' for integers, real numbers, and complex numbers. For the real numbers, for all $a \in \mathbb{R}$,

$$0 + a = a,$$

$$a + 0 = a, \text{ and}$$

$$0 + 0 = 0.$$

Similarly, The number 1 is the 'multiplicative _____' for integers, real numbers, and complex numbers.

a. Action
b. Intersection
c. Identity
d. ARIA

14. The _____ are the set of numbers consisting of the natural numbers including 0 and their negatives. They are numbers that can be written without a fractional or decimal component, and fall within the set {... −2, −1, 0, 1, 2, ...}.
a. A Mathematical Theory of Communication
b. Integers
c. A posteriori
d. A chemical equation

15. The '_____' puzzle consists of four cubes with faces colored with four colors. The object of the puzzle is to stack these cubes in a column so that each side of the stack shows each of the four colors. The distribution of colors on each cube is unique.

Chapter 3. Functions

a. Eulerian path
b. Instant Insanity
c. Independent set
d. Induced path

16. In mathematics, the _____ of a number n is the number that, when added to n, yields zero. The _____ of n is denoted −n. For example, 7 is −7, because 7 + (−7) = 0, and the _____ of −0.3 is 0.3, because −0.3 + 0.3 = 0.
    a. Associativity
    b. Arity
    c. Algebraic structure
    d. Additive inverse

17. In mathematics, _____ is a property that a binary operation can have. It means that, within an expression containing two or more of the same associative operators in a row, the order that the operations are performed does not matter as long as the sequence of the operands is not changed. That is, rearranging the parentheses in such an expression will not change its value.
    a. Unital
    b. Algebraically closed
    c. Associativity
    d. Idempotence

18. In mathematics, a _____ is a convincing demonstration that some mathematical statement is necessarily true. _____s are obtained from deductive reasoning, rather than from inductive or empirical arguments. That is, a _____ must demonstrate that a statement is true in all cases, without a single exception.
    a. Congruent
    b. Germ
    c. Conchoid
    d. Proof

19. In mathematics, the _____ of a set is a measure of the 'number of elements of the set'. For example, the set A = {1, 2, 3} contains 3 elements, and therefore A has a _____ of 3. There are two approaches to _____ - one which compares sets directly using bijections and injections, and another which uses cardinal numbers.
    a. 1-center problem
    b. 2-3 heap
    c. 120-cell
    d. Cardinality

Chapter 3. Functions

20. In abstract algebra, a _____ is an algebraic structure in which the operations of addition, subtraction, multiplication and division may be performed in a way that satisfies some familiar rules from the arithmetic of ordinary numbers.

All _____s are rings, but not conversely. _____s differ from rings most importantly in the requirement that division be possible, but also, in modern definitions, by the requirement that the multiplication operation in a _____ be commutative.

   a. Chord
   b. Field
   c. Blind
   d. Functional

21. In abstract algebra, a _____ or Galois field is a field that contains only finitely many elements. _____s are important in number theory, algebraic geometry, Galois theory, cryptography, and coding theory. The _____s are completely known.
   a. Frobenius endomorphism
   b. 1-center problem
   c. Network coding
   d. Finite Field

22. _____ is the mathematical operation of scaling one number by another. It is one of the four basic operations in elementary arithmetic.

_____ is defined for whole numbers in terms of repeated addition; for example, 4 multiplied by 3 can be calculated by adding 3 copies of 4 together:

$$4 + 4 + 4 = 12.$$

_____ of rational numbers and real numbers is defined by systematic generalization of this basic idea.

   a. The number 0 is even.
   b. Least common multiple
   c. Highest common factor
   d. Multiplication

23. _____ is a systematic method for multiplying two numbers that does not require the multiplication table, only the ability to multiply and divide by 2, and to add. Also known as Egyptian multiplication and Peasant multiplication, it decomposes one of the multiplicands into a sum of powers of two and creates a table of doublings of the second multiplicand. This method may be called mediation and duplation, where mediation means halving one number and duplation means doubling the other number.

 a. A posteriori
 b. A chemical equation
 c. A Mathematical Theory of Communication
 d. Ancient Egyptian multiplication

24. In mathematics, the word _____ has at least two distinct meanings, outlined in the sections below. For other uses see _____.

The term the _____ sometimes denotes the real line.

 a. Barrelled spaces
 b. Coordinate rotations and reflections
 c. Christofides heuristics algorithm
 d. Continuum

25. In mathematics, the _____ is a hypothesis, advanced by Georg Cantor, about the possible sizes of infinite sets. Cantor introduced the concept of cardinality to compare the sizes of infinite sets, and he gave two proofs that the cardinality of the set of integers is strictly smaller than that of the set of real numbers. His proofs, however, give no indication of the extent to which the cardinality of the natural numbers is less than that of the real numbers.

 a. Closed under some operation
 b. Blotto game
 c. Compact groups
 d. Continuum hypothesis

Chapter 4. The Integers

1. In mathematics, a set is said to be _____ if the operation on members of the set produces a member of the set. For example, the real numbers are closed under subtraction, but the natural numbers are not: 3 and 7 are both natural numbers, but the result of 3 − 7 is not.

   Similarly, a set is said to be closed under a collection of operations if it is closed under each of the operations individually.

   a. Contingency table
   b. Closed under some operation
   c. Control chart
   d. Continuous linear extension

2. In mathematics, an _____ in the sense of ring theory is a subring $\mathcal{O}$ of a ring R that satisfies the conditions

   1. R is a ring which is a finite-dimensional algebra over the rational number field $\mathbb{Q}$
   2. $\mathcal{O}$ spans R over $\mathbb{Q}$, so that $\mathbb{Q}\mathcal{O} = R$, and
   3. $\mathcal{O}$ is a lattice in R.

   The third condition can be stated more accurately, in terms of the extension of scalars of R to the real numbers, embedding R in a real vector space. In less formal terms, additively $\mathcal{O}$ should be a free abelian group generated by a basis for R over $\mathbb{Q}$.

   The leading example is the case where R is a number field K and $\mathcal{O}$ is its ring of integers. In algebraic number theory there are examples for any K other than the rational field of proper subrings of the ring of integers that are also _____ s.

   a. Order
   b. Efficiency
   c. Algebraic
   d. Annihilator

3. The '_____' puzzle consists of four cubes with faces colored with four colors. The object of the puzzle is to stack these cubes in a column so that each side of the stack shows each of the four colors. The distribution of colors on each cube is unique.
   a. Instant Insanity
   b. Eulerian path
   c. Induced path
   d. Independent set

Chapter 4. The Integers

4. _____ is an abbreviation of the Latin phrase 'quod erat demonstrandum' which means literally, 'that which was to be demonstrated'. The phrase is written in its abbreviated form at the end of a mathematical proof or philosophical argument, to signify that the last statement deduced was the one to be demonstrated, so the proof is complete.

The phrase is a translation into Latin of the original Greek á½…περ á¼"δει δειξαι. (hoper edei deixai) which was used by many early mathematicians including Euclid and Archimedes.

  a. Proofs from THE BOOK
  b. Q.E.D.
  c. Nonconstructive proof
  d. Direct proof

5. In mathematics, the _____ states that every non-empty set of positive integers contains a smallest element.

The phrase '_____' is sometimes taken to be synonymous with the 'well-ordering theorem'. On other occasions it is understood to be the proposition that the set of integers {..., -2, -1, 0, 1, 2, 3, ...} contains a well-ordered subset, called the natural numbers, in which every nonempty subset contains a least element.

  a. 1-center problem
  b. 2-3 heap
  c. 120-cell
  d. Well-Ordering Principle

6. In mathematics, _____ is a property that a binary operation can have. It means that, within an expression containing two or more of the same associative operators in a row, the order that the operations are performed does not matter as long as the sequence of the operands is not changed. That is, rearranging the parentheses in such an expression will not change its value.
  a. Idempotence
  b. Algebraically closed
  c. Associativity
  d. Unital

7. In mathematics, a _____ is a calculation involving two operands, in other words, an operation whose arity is two. _____s can be accomplished using either a binary function or binary operator. _____s are sometimes called dyadic operations in order to avoid confusion with the binary numeral system.

Chapter 4. The Integers

a. Binary operation
b. 2-3 heap
c. 1-center problem
d. 120-cell

8. In mathematics, and in particular in abstract algebra, distributivity is a property of binary operations that generalises the _____ law from elementary algebra.
   a. Distributive
   b. General linear group
   c. Closure with a twist
   d. Permutation

9. In mathematics, the term _____ has several different important meanings:

   - An _____ is an equality that remains true regardless of the values of any variables that appear within it, to distinguish it from an equality which is true under more particular conditions. For this, the 'triple bar' symbol ≡ is sometimes used.
   - In algebra, an _____ or _____ element of a set S with a binary operation Â· is an element e that, when combined with any element x of S, produces that same x. That is, eÂ·x = xÂ·e = x for all x in S.
     o The _____ function from a set S to itself, often denoted id or id$_S$, s the function such that i = x for all x in S. This function serves as the _____ element in the set of all functions from S to itself with respect to function composition.
     o In linear algebra, the _____ matrix of size n is the n-by-n square matrix with ones on the main diagonal and zeros elsewhere. This matrix serves as the _____ with respect to matrix multiplication.

A common example of the first meaning is the trigonometric _____

$$\sin^2 \theta + \cos^2 \theta = 1$$

which is true for all real values of θ, as opposed to

$$\cos \theta = 1,$$

which is true only for some values of θ, not all. For example, the latter equation is true when $\theta = 0$, false when $\theta = 2$

The concepts of 'additive _____' and 'multiplicative _____' are central to the Peano axioms. The number 0 is the 'additive _____' for integers, real numbers, and complex numbers. For the real numbers, for all $a \in \mathbb{R}$,

$$0 + a = a,$$

$$a + 0 = a, \text{ and}$$

$$0 + 0 = 0.$$

Similarly, The number 1 is the 'multiplicative _____' for integers, real numbers, and complex numbers.

a. Action
b. Identity
c. ARIA
d. Intersection

10. In mathematics, a _____ is the end result of a division problem. It can also be expressed as the number of times the divisor divides into the dividend.

a. Notation
b. Limiting
c. Marginal cost
d. Quotient

11. In mathematics, the _____ is a direct product of sets. The _____ is named after René Descartes, whose formulation of analytic geometry gave rise to this concept.

Specifically, the _____ of two sets X and Y, denoted X × Y, is the set of all possible ordered pairs whose first component is a member of X and whose second component is a member of Y:

$$X \times Y = \{(x,y) | x \in X \text{ and } y \in Y\}.$$

For example, the _____ of the 13-element set of standard playing card ranks {Ace, King, Queen, Jack, 10, 9, 8, 7, 6, 5, 4, 3, 2} and the four-element set of card suits {â™ , â™¥, â™¦, â™£} is the 52-element set of all possible playing cards ,, ...,,, ...,}.

a. Cartesian product
b. Set of all sets
c. Choice function
d. Disjoint sets

12. In mathematics, a _____ is a statement that can be proved on the basis of explicitly stated or previously agreed assumptions.
    a. Logical value
    b. Boolean function
    c. Disjunction introduction
    d. Theorem

13. In mathematics, computing, linguistics and related subjects, an _____ is a sequence of finite instructions, often used for calculation and data processing. It is formally a type of effective method in which a list of well-defined instructions for completing a task will, when given an initial state, proceed through a well-defined series of successive states, eventually terminating in an end-state. The transition from one state to the next is not necessarily deterministic; some _____s, known as probabilistic _____s, incorporate randomness.
    a. Algorithm
    b. Approximate counting algorithm
    c. Out-of-core
    d. In-place algorithm

14. In mathematics and computer science, the _____ and ceiling functions map real numbers to the next lower and next higher integers.

The _____ function of a real number x, sometimes called the greatest integer or entier function, and denoted variously by [x] $\lfloor x \rfloor$, _____(x), or int(x), is a function whose value is the largest integer less than or equal to x. Formally, for all real numbers x,

$$\lfloor x \rfloor = \max\{n \in \mathbb{Z} \mid n \leq x\}.$$

For example, _____(2.9) = 2, _____(−2) = −2 and _____(−12/5) = −3.

a. Floor
b. 120-cell
c. 1-center problem
d. 2-3 heap

Chapter 4. The Integers

15. In mathematics, a _____ is a convincing demonstration that some mathematical statement is necessarily true. _____s are obtained from deductive reasoning, rather than from inductive or empirical arguments. That is, a _____ must demonstrate that a statement is true in all cases, without a single exception.

   a. Conchoid
   b. Proof
   c. Congruent
   d. Germ

16. In mathematics and computer science, _____ (also base-16, hexa or base, of 16. It uses sixteen distinct symbols, most often the symbols 0-9 to represent values zero to nine, and A, B, C, D, E, F (or a through f) to represent values ten to fifteen.

   Its primary use is as a human friendly representation of binary coded values, so it is often used in digital electronics and computer engineering.

   a. Hexadecimal
   b. Factoradic
   c. Radix
   d. Tetradecimal

17. In computational complexity theory, the complexity class _____ is a class of problems having two properties:

   - Any given solution to the problem can be verified quickly; the set of problems with this property is called NP.
   - If the problem can be solved quickly, then so can every problem in NP.

   Although any given solution to such a problem can be verified quickly, there is no known efficient way to locate a solution in the first place; indeed, the most notable characteristic of _____ problems is that no fast solution to them is known. That is, the time required to solve the problem using any currently known algorithm increases very quickly as the size of the problem grows. As a result, the time required to solve even moderately large versions of many of these problems easily reaches into the billions or trillions of years, using any amount of computing power available today. As a consequence, determining whether or not it is possible to solve these problems quickly is one of the principal unsolved problems in computer science today.

   a. Subset sum
   b. 3-partition problem
   c. NP-complete
   d. Quadratic assignment problem

Chapter 4. The Integers

18. The _____ numeral system is the base-8 number system, and uses the digits 0 to 7. Numerals can be made from binary numerals by grouping consecutive digits into groups of three (starting from the right.) For example, the binary representation for decimal 74 is 1001010, which groups into 001 001 010 -- so the _____ representation is 112.

   a. A posteriori
   b. A chemical equation
   c. A Mathematical Theory of Communication
   d. Octal

19. In mathematics, a _____ of an integer n is an integer which evenly divides n without leaving a remainder.

For example, 7 is a _____ of 42 because 42/7 = 6. We also say 42 is divisible by 7 or 42 is a multiple of 7 or 7 divides 42 or 7 is a factor of 42 and we usually write 7 | 42.

   a. 1-center problem
   b. 2-3 heap
   c. 120-cell
   d. Divisor

20. In mathematics, the _____, sometimes known as the greatest common factor or highest common factor, of two non-zero integers, is the largest positive integer that divides both numbers without remainder.

This notion can be extended to polynomials, see _____ of two polynomials.

The _____ of a and b is written as gc, or sometimes simply as.

   a. Minuend
   b. Multiplication
   c. Highest common factor
   d. Greatest common divisor

21. In number theory, the _____ is an algorithm to determine the greatest common divisor of two elements of any Euclidean domain. Its major significance is that it does not require factoring the two integers, and it is also significant in that it is one of the oldest algorithms known, dating back to the ancient Greeks.

The _____ is one of the oldest algorithms known, since it appeared in Euclid's Elements around 300 BC.

a. A posteriori
b. A chemical equation
c. A Mathematical Theory of Communication
d. Euclidean algorithm

22. In combinatorial mathematics, a _____ is an un-ordered collection of distinct elements, usually of a prescribed size and taken from a given set. Given such a set S, a _____ of elements of S is just a subset of S, where as always forsets the order of the elements is not taken into account. Also, as always forsets, no elements can be repeated more than once in a _____; this is often referred to as a 'collection without repetition'.

a. Fill-in
b. Sparsity
c. Heawood number
d. Combination

23. In mathematics, _____ are a concept central to linear algebra and related fields of mathematics

Suppose that K is a field and V is a vector space over K.

a. Linear combinations
b. Setoid
c. Linear span
d. Polarization

24. In mathematics, a _____ is a natural number which has exactly two distinct natural number divisors: 1 and itself. An infinitude of _____s exists, as demonstrated by Euclid around 300 BC. The first twenty-five _____s are:

2, 3, 5, 7, 11, 13, 17, 19, 23, 29, 31, 37, 41, 43, 47, 53, 59, 61, 67, 71, 73, 79, 83, 89, 97.

a. Prime number
b. Pronic number
c. Highly composite number
d. Perrin number

25. In mathematics, especially in geometry and group theory, a _____ in R^n is a discrete subgroup of R^n which spans the real vector space R^n. Every _____ in R^n can be generated from a basis for the vector space by forming all linear combinations with integral coefficients. A _____ may be viewed as a regular tiling of a space by a primitive cell.

a. Group
b. Homogeneity
c. Boundary
d. Lattice

26. In arithmetic and number theory, the _____ or lowest common multiple or smallest common multiple of two integers a and b is the smallest positive integer that is a multiple of both a and b. Since it is a multiple, it can be divided by a and b without a remainder. If either a or b is 0, so that there is no such positive integer, then lc is defined to be zero.
    a. Least common multiple
    b. Lowest common denominator
    c. Plus and minus signs
    d. Plus-minus sign

27. A _____ is a 2D geometric symbolic representation of information according to some visualization technique. Sometimes, the technique uses a 3D visualization which is then projected onto the 2D surface. The word graph is sometimes used as a synonym for _____.
    a. 1-center problem
    b. Diagram
    c. 2-3 heap
    d. 120-cell

28. A _____ number is a positive integer which has a positive divisor other than one or itself. By definition, every integer greater than one is either a prime number or a _____ number.zero and one are considered to be neither prime nor _____. For example, the integer 14 is a _____ number because it can be factored as 2 × 7.
    a. Discontinuity
    b. Composite
    c. Key server
    d. Basis

29. In mathematics, given a subset S of a partially ordered set T, the supremum (sup) of S, if it exists, is the least element of T that is greater than or equal to each element of S. Consequently, the supremum is also referred to as the _____, lub or _____. If the supremum exists, it may or may not belong to S.
    a. Least upper bound
    b. Supermodular
    c. Complete Heyting algebra
    d. Compact element

30. In mathematics, especially in order theory, an _____ of a subset S of some partially ordered set is an element of P which is greater than or equal to every element of S. The term lower bound is defined dually as an element of P which is lesser than or equal to every element of S. A set with an _____ is said to be bounded from above by that bound, a set with a lower bound is said to be bounded from below by that bound.
   a. Upper bound
   b. Infinite descending chain
   c. Order-embedding
   d. Order isomorphism

31. In mathematics, the _____ is a simple, ancient algorithm for finding all prime numbers up to a specified integer. It works efficiently for the smaller primes. It was created by Eratosthenes, an ancient Greek mathematician.
   a. 2-3 heap
   b. 120-cell
   c. Sieve of Eratosthenes
   d. 1-center problem

32. In number theory, the _____ states that every natural number greater than 1 can be written as a unique product of prime numbers. For instance,

$$6936 = 2^3 \times 3 \times 17^2,$$

$$1200 = 2^4 \times 3 \times 5^2.$$

There are no other possible factorizations of 6936 or 1200 into non-negative prime numbers. The above representation collapses repeated prime factors into powers for easier identification.

   a. Cyclic number
   b. Feit–Thompson theorem
   c. Fundamental Theorem of Arithmetic
   d. Dedekind sums

33. _____ IPA: [pjɛʁ ɛ dəmfɛʁ 'ma] (17 August 1601 or 1607/8 - 12 January 1665) was a French lawyer at the Parlement of Toulouse, France, and a mathematician who is given credit for early developments that led to modern calculus. In particular, he is recognized for his discovery of an original method of finding the greatest and the smallest ordinates of curved lines, which is analogous to that of the then unknown differential calculus, as well as his research into the theory of numbers. He also made notable contributions to analytic geometry, probability, and optics.

a. Philip J. Davis
b. Nikita Borisov
c. Pierre de Fermat
d. Felix Hausdorff

34. In number theory, the _____ describes the asymptotic distribution of the prime numbers. The _____ gives a rough description of how the primes are distributed.

Roughly speaking, the _____ states that if you randomly select a number nearby some large number N, the chance of it being prime is about 1 / ln(N), where ln(N) denotes the natural logarithm of N.

a. Sieve theory
b. Mahler measure
c. Prime-counting function
d. Prime Number Theorem

35. In mathematics, a _____ is a mathematical statement which appears resourceful, but has not been formally proven to be true under the rules of mathematical logic. Once a _____ is formally proven true it is elevated to the status of theorem and may be used afterwards without risk in the construction of other formal mathematical proofs. Until that time, mathematicians may use the _____ on a provisional basis, but any resulting work is itself provisional until the underlying _____ is cleared up.
a. Heawood conjecture
b. Whitehead conjecture
c. Moral certainty
d. Conjecture

36. In mathematics the infimum of a subset of some set is the greatest element, not necessarily in the subset, that is less than or equal to all elements of the subset. Consequently the term _____ is also commonly used. Infima of real numbers are a common special case that is especially important in analysis.
a. Supremum
b. Strict weak ordering
c. Strong antichain
d. Greatest lower bound

37. In mathematics, especially in order theory, an upper bound of a subset S of some partially ordered set is an element of P which is greater than or equal to every element of S. The term _____ is defined dually as an element of P which is lesser than or equal to every element of S. A set with an upper bound is said to be bounded from above by that bound, a set with a _____ is said to be bounded from below by that bound.

42   Chapter 4. The Integers

   a. Monomial order
   b. Lower bound
   c. Cofinality
   d. Partially ordered set

38. The _____ is a famous unsolved problem in number theory that involves prime numbers. It states:

   There are infinitely many primes p such that p + 2 is also prime.

Such a pair of prime numbers is called a prime twin. The conjecture has been researched by many number theorists.

   a. Legendre sieve
   b. Character sum
   c. Prime number theorem
   d. Twin prime conjecture

39. In set theory and its applications throughout mathematics, a _____ is a collection of sets that can be unambiguously defined by a property that all its members share. The precise definition of '_____' depends on foundational context. In work on ZF set theory, the notion of _____ is informal, whereas other set theories, such as NBG set theory, axiomatize the notion of '_____'.
   a. Filter
   b. Congruent
   c. Coherence
   d. Class

40. As an abstract term, _____ means similarity between objects.
   a. Congruence
   b. 2-3 heap
   c. 1-center problem
   d. 120-cell

41. In geometry, two sets of points are called _____ if one can be transformed into the other by an isometry. Less formally, two figures are _____ if they have the same shape and size, but are in different positions.

In a Euclidean system, congruence is fundamental; it is the counterpart of equality for numbers.

a. Gamma test
b. Germ
c. Function
d. Congruent

42. In mathematics, given a set X and an equivalence relation ~ on X, the _____ of an element a in X is the subset of all elements in X which are equivalent to a:

$$[a] = \{x \in X | x \sim a\}.$$

The notion of _____ es is useful for constructing sets out of already constructed ones. The set of all _____ es in X given an equivalence relation ~ is usually denoted as X / ~ and called the quotient set of X by ~. This operation can be thought of as the act of 'dividing' the input set by the equivalence relation, hence both the name 'quotient', and the notation, which are both reminiscent of division.

a. A chemical equation
b. A Mathematical Theory of Communication
c. Equivalence relation
d. Equivalence class

43. In number theory, a _____ of a positive integer n is a way of writing n as a sum of positive integers. Two sums which only differ in the order of their summands are considered to be the same _____; if order matters then the sum becomes a composition. A summand in a _____ is also called a part.
a. Derivative algebra
b. Distribution
c. Congruent
d. Partition

44. The word _____ is the Latin ablative of modulus which itself means 'a small measure.' It was introduced into mathematics in the book Disquisitiones Arithmeticae by Carl Friedrich Gauss in 1801. Ever since, however, '_____' has gained many meanings, some exact and some imprecise.

- (This usage is from Gauss's book.) Given the integers a, b and n, the expression a ≡ b (mod n) means that a − b is a multiple of n, or equivalently, a and b both leave the same remainder when divided by n. For more details, see modular arithmetic.

- In computing, given two numbers (either integer or real), a and n, a _____ n is the remainder after numerical division of a by n, under certain constraints. See _____ operation.

a. Per mil
b. Quotition
c. Modulo
d. Predictor-corrector method

45. The _____ is a unique, numerical commercial book identifier, based upon the 9-digit Standard Book Numbering code created in the UK by the booksellers and stationers W.H. Smith and others in 1966. The 10-digit _____ format was developed by the International Organization for Standardization and published as an international standard, ISO 2108, in 1970. Currently, the ISO TC 46/SC 9 is responsible for the standard.
a. ISBN
b. A Mathematical Theory of Communication
c. A posteriori
d. A chemical equation

46. A _____ is a form of redundancy check used for error detection, the decimal equivalent of a binary checksum. It consists of a single digit computed from the other digits in the message.

With a _____, one can detect simple errors in the input of a series of digits, such as a single mistyped digit, or the permutation of two successive digits.

a. Forward error correction
b. Data scrubbing
c. Summation check
d. Check digit

47. In information theory, a _____ is a function mapping an alphabet to non-negative real numbers, satisfying a generalization of Kraft's inequality. A _____ page, a type of character encoding table, is one such _____.
a. File Camouflage
b. Link encryption
c. Code
d. Deterministic encryption

48. In mathematics, the _____ is an operation which takes two vectors over the real numbers R and returns a real-valued scalar quantity. It is the standard inner product of the orthonormal Euclidean space.

The _____ of two vectors a = [$a_1, a_2, \ldots, a_n$] and b = [$b_1, b_2, \ldots, b_n$] is defined as:

$$\mathbf{a} \cdot \mathbf{b} = \sum_{i=1}^{n} a_i b_i = a_1 b_1 + a_2 b_2 + \cdots + a_n b_n$$

where Σ denotes summation notation and n is the dimension of the vectors.

a. Principal axis theorem
b. Conjugate transpose
c. Matrix determinant lemma
d. Dot product

49. The _____ is a barcode symbology, that is widely used in the United States and Canada for tracking trade items in stores. In the _____-A barcode, each digit is represented by a seven-bit sequence, encoded by a series of alternating bars and spaces. Guard bars, shown in green, separate the two groups of six digits.

The _____ encodes 12 decimal digits as SLLLLLLMRRRRRRE, where S and E are the bit pattern 101, M is the bit pattern 01010, and each L and R are digits, each one represented by a seven-bit code.

a. A chemical equation
b. A posteriori
c. Universal product code
d. A Mathematical Theory of Communication

50. In physics and in _____ calculus, a _____ is a concept characterized by a magnitude and a direction. A _____ can be thought of as an arrow in Euclidean space, drawn from an initial point A pointing to a terminal point B.
a. Dominance
b. Deviation
c. Constraint
d. Vector

51. _____ is a theoretical computer scientist and professor of computer science and molecular biology at the University of Southern California. He is known for being a co-inventor of the RSA cryptosystem in 1977, and of DNA computing. RSA is in widespread use in security applications, including https.

a. William Kingdon Clifford
b. Johann Karl August Radon
c. Leonard Max Adleman
d. Harold Hall 'Doc' Keen

52. _____ is an Israeli cryptographer. He was one of the inventors of the RSA algorithm, one of the inventors of the Feige-Fiat-Shamir Identification Scheme, one of the inventors of differential cryptanalysis and has made numerous contributions to the fields of cryptography and computer science.

Born in Tel Aviv, Shamir received a BS in Mathematics from Tel Aviv University in 1973 and obtained his MSc and PhD in Computer Science from the Weizmann Institute in 1975 and 1977 respectively.

a. Ernst Friedrich Ferdinand Zermelo
b. Adi Shamir
c. Edwin Thompson Jaynes
d. Iain S. Duff

Chapter 5. Induction and Recursion

1. _____ is a method of mathematical proof typically used to establish that a given statement is true of all natural numbers. It is done by proving that the first statement in the infinite sequence of statements is true, and then proving that if any one statement in the infinite sequence of statements is true, then so is the next one.

The method can be extended to prove statements about more general well-founded structures, such as trees; this generalization, known as structural induction, is used in mathematical logic and computer science.

   a. Herbrand structure
   b. Finitary
   c. Ground expression
   d. Mathematical induction

2. In mathematics, the _____ of a non-negative integer n, denoted by n!, is the product of all positive integers less than or equal to n. For example,

$$5! = 1 \times 2 \times 3 \times 4 \times 5 = 120$$

and
$$6! = 1 \times 2 \times 3 \times 4 \times 5 \times 6 = 720$$

The notation n! was introduced by Christian Kramp in 1808.

The _____ function is formally defined by

$$n! = \prod_{k=1}^{n} k \qquad \forall n \in \mathbb{N}.$$

The above definition incorporates the instance

$$0! = 1$$

as an instance of the fact that the product of no numbers at all is 1.

   a. Factorial
   b. Plane partition
   c. Symbolic combinatorics
   d. Partition of a set

3. In mathematics and in the sciences, a _____ (plural: _____e, formulæ or _____s) is a concise way of expressing information symbolically (as in a mathematical or chemical _____), or a general relationship between quantities. One of many famous _____e is Albert Einstein's E = mc² (see special relativity

In mathematics, a _____ is a key to solve an equation with variables. For example, the problem of determining the volume of a sphere is one that requires a significant amount of integral calculus to solve.

a. 2-3 heap
b. Formula
c. 120-cell
d. 1-center problem

4. In number theory, the _____ states that every natural number greater than 1 can be written as a unique product of prime numbers. For instance,

$$6936 = 2^3 \times 3 \times 17^2,$$
$$1200 = 2^4 \times 3 \times 5^2.$$

There are no other possible factorizations of 6936 or 1200 into non-negative prime numbers. The above representation collapses repeated prime factors into powers for easier identification.

a. Feit–Thompson theorem
b. Dedekind sums
c. Cyclic number
d. Fundamental Theorem of Arithmetic

5. In mathematics, a _____ is a statement that can be proved on the basis of explicitly stated or previously agreed assumptions.
a. Boolean function
b. Logical value
c. Disjunction introduction
d. Theorem

6. In mathematics, the _____ states that every non-empty set of positive integers contains a smallest element.

The phrase '_____' is sometimes taken to be synonymous with the 'well-ordering theorem'. On other occasions it is understood to be the proposition that the set of integers {..., -2, -1, 0, 1, 2, 3, ...} contains a well-ordered subset, called the natural numbers, in which every nonempty subset contains a least element.

Chapter 5. Induction and Recursion

a. 120-cell
b. 1-center problem
c. 2-3 heap
d. Well-Ordering Principle

7. In combinatorial mathematics, a _____ is an un-ordered collection of distinct elements, usually of a prescribed size and taken from a given set. Given such a set S, a _____ of elements of S is just a subset of S, where as always forsets the order of the elements is not taken into account. Also, as always forsets, no elements can be repeated more than once in a _____; this is often referred to as a 'collection without repetition'.

a. Sparsity
b. Heawood number
c. Fill-in
d. Combination

8. In mathematics, _____ are a concept central to linear algebra and related fields of mathematics

Suppose that K is a field and V is a vector space over K.

a. Linear combinations
b. Linear span
c. Setoid
d. Polarization

9. In mathematics, a real-valued function f defined on an interval is called _____, concave upwards, concave up or _____ cup, if for any two points x and y in its domain C and any t in [0,1], we have

$$f(tx + (1-t)y) \leq tf(x) + (1-t)f(y).$$

_____ function on an interval.

In other words, a function is _____ if and only if its epigraph is a _____ set.

Pictorially, a function is called '_____' if the function lies below the straight line segment connecting two points, for any two points in the interval.

A function is called strictly _____ if

$$f(tx + (1-t)y) < tf(x) + (1-t)f(y)$$

for any t in and $x \neq y$.

A function f is said to be concave if − f is _____.

a. Convex
b. Contrapositive
c. Continuum
d. Continuous wavelet

10. In ring theory, a branch of abstract algebra, an _____ is a special subset of a ring. The _____ concept generalizes in an appropriate way some important properties of integers like 'even number' or 'multiple of 3'.

For instance, in rings one studies prime _____s instead of prime numbers, one defines coprime _____s as a generalization of coprime numbers, and one can prove a generalized Chinese remainder theorem about _____s.

a. Equity
b. Equaliser
c. Element
d. Ideal

11. In mathematics, a _____ is a natural number which has exactly two distinct natural number divisors: 1 and itself. An infinitude of _____s exists, as demonstrated by Euclid around 300 BC. The first twenty-five _____s are:

2, 3, 5, 7, 11, 13, 17, 19, 23, 29, 31, 37, 41, 43, 47, 53, 59, 61, 67, 71, 73, 79, 83, 89, 97.

a. Highly composite number
b. Perrin number
c. Pronic number
d. Prime number

12. A _____ or inductive definition is one that defines something in terms of itself, albeit in a useful way. For it to work, the definition in any given case must be well-founded, avoiding an infinite regress.

In simple terms, the _____ is one that grows an awareness and clarity upon itself toward a conclusive end, with each recurrence contributing something new toward the end definition.

Chapter 5. Induction and Recursion

a. 1-center problem
b. 2-3 heap
c. 120-cell
d. Recursive definition

13. Initial objects are also called _____, and terminal objects are also called final.
a. Colimit
b. Direct limit
c. Terminal object
d. Coterminal

14. In mathematics, a _____ is an equation that defines a sequence recursively: each term of the sequence is defined as a function of the preceding terms.

A difference equation is a specific type of _____.

An example of a _____ is the logistic map:

$$x_{n+1} = rx_n(1 - x_n).$$

Some simply defined _____s can have very complex behaviours and are sometimes studied by physicists and mathematicians in a field of mathematics known as nonlinear analysis.

a. Recurrence relation
b. Topological module
c. Hecke algebra
d. Theory of equations

15. In mathematics, an arithmetic progression or _____ is a sequence of numbers such that the difference of any two successive members of the sequence is a constant. For instance, the sequence 3, 5, 7, 9, 11, 13... is an arithmetic progression with common difference 2.
a. Alternating series test
b. Eisenstein series
c. Arithmetic sequence
d. Edgeworth series

Chapter 5. Induction and Recursion

16. Leonardo of Pisa (c. 1170 - c. 1250), also known as Leonardo Pisano, Leonardo Bonacci, Leonardo _____, or, most commonly, simply _____, was an Italian mathematician, considered by some 'the most talented mathematician of the Middle Ages'.
    a. Harry Hinsley
    b. Ralph C. Merkle
    c. Fibonacci
    d. Guido Castelnuovo

17. In statistics, _____ has two related meanings:

    - the arithmetic _____.
    - the expected value of a random variable, which is also called the population _____.

    It is sometimes stated that the '_____' _____s average. This is incorrect if '_____' is taken in the specific sense of 'arithmetic _____' as there are different types of averages: the _____, median, and mode. For instance, average house prices almost always use the median value for the average.

    For a real-valued random variable X, the _____ is the expectation of X.

    a. Mean
    b. Statistical population
    c. Proportional hazards model
    d. Probability

18. In geometry, a _____ is a convex regular polyhedron. These are the three-dimensional analogs of the convex regular polygons. There are precisely five such figures.
    a. 1-center problem
    b. 2-3 heap
    c. 120-cell
    d. Platonic solid

19. The mathematical concept of a _____ expresses the intuitive idea of deterministic dependence between two quantities, one of which is viewed as primary and the other as secondary. A _____ then is a way to associate a unique output for each input of a specified type, for example, a real number or an element of a given set.
    a. Going up
    b. Coherent
    c. Grill
    d. Function

Chapter 5. Induction and Recursion

20. In mathematics, an _____ in the sense of ring theory is a subring $\mathcal{O}$ of a ring R that satisfies the conditions

   1. R is a ring which is a finite-dimensional algebra over the rational number field $\mathbb{Q}$
   2. $\mathcal{O}$ spans R over $\mathbb{Q}$, so that $\mathbb{Q}\mathcal{O} = R$, and
   3. $\mathcal{O}$ is a lattice in R.

The third condition can be stated more accurately, in terms of the extension of scalars of R to the real numbers, embedding R in a real vector space. In less formal terms, additively $\mathcal{O}$ should be a free abelian group generated by a basis for R over $\mathbb{Q}$.

The leading example is the case where R is a number field K and $\mathcal{O}$ is its ring of integers. In algebraic number theory there are examples for any K other than the rational field of proper subrings of the ring of integers that are also _____ s.

   a. Order
   b. Efficiency
   c. Annihilator
   d. Algebraic

21. In mathematics, the _____ of a ring R, often denoted cha, is defined to be the smallest number of times one must add the ring's multiplicative identity element to itself to get the additive identity element; the ring is said to have _____ zero if this repeated sum never reaches the additive identity. That is, cha is the smallest positive number n such that

$$\underbrace{1 + \cdots + 1}_{n \text{ summands}} = 0$$

if such a number n exists, and 0 otherwise. The _____ may also be taken to be the exponent of the ring's additive group, that is, the smallest positive n such that

$$\underbrace{a + \cdots + a}_{n \text{ summands}} = 0$$

for every element a of the ring.

   a. Class
   b. Coherent
   c. Disk
   d. Characteristic

Chapter 5. Induction and Recursion

22. In linear algebra, one associates a polynomial to every square matrix, its _____. This polynomial encodes several important properties of the matrix, most notably its eigenvalues, its determinant and its trace.

Given a square matrix A, we want to find a polynomial whose roots are precisely the eigenvalues of A.

   a. Polynomial long division
   b. Coefficient
   c. Littlewood polynomial
   d. Characteristic polynomial

23. In mathematics, a _____ is an expression constructed from variables and constants, using the operations of addition, subtraction, multiplication, and constant non-negative whole number exponents. For example, $x^2 - 4x + 7$ is a _____, but $x^2 - 4/x + 7x^{3/2}$ is not, because its second term involves division by the variable x and also because its third term contains an exponent that is not a whole number.

_____s are one of the most important concepts in algebra and throughout mathematics and science.

   a. Coimage
   b. Semifield
   c. Group extension
   d. Polynomial

24. In vascular plants, the _____ is the organ of a plant body that typically lies below the surface of the soil. This is not always the case, however, since a _____ can also be aerial (that is, growing above the ground) or aerating (that is, growing up above the ground or especially above water.) Furthermore, a stem normally occurring below ground is not exceptional either
   a. Root
   b. 120-cell
   c. 2-3 heap
   d. 1-center problem

25. The Tower of Hanoi or _____ is a mathematical game or puzzle. It consists of three rods, and a number of disks of different sizes which can slide onto any rod. The puzzle starts with the disks neatly stacked in order of size on one rod, the smallest at the top, thus making a conical shape.
   a. 1-center problem
   b. 120-cell
   c. 2-3 heap
   d. Towers of Hanoi

Chapter 5. Induction and Recursion

26. In mathematics a _____ is a formal power series whose coefficients encode information about a sequence a_n that is indexed by the natural numbers.

There are various types of _____s, including ordinary _____s, exponential _____s, Lambert series, Bell series, and Dirichlet series; definitions and examples are given below. Every sequence has a _____ of each type.

- a. Rule of sum
- b. Restricted sumset
- c. Combinatorial design
- d. Generating function

27. In algebra, the _____ decomposition or _____ expansion is used to reduce the degree of either the numerator or the denominator of a rational function. The outcome of _____ expansion expresses that function as a sum of fractions, where:

- the denominator of each term is a power of an irreducible polynomial and
- the numerator is a polynomial of smaller degree than that irreducible polynomial.

See _____s in integration for an account of their use in finding antiderivatives. They are also used in calculating the inverse of transforms; such as the Laplace transform, or the Z-transform.

The basic idea behind _____s is to work backwards to separate a function.

- a. Concept algebra
- b. Continuant
- c. Partial fraction
- d. Real structure

Chapter 6. Principles of Counting

1. In probability theory, an _____ is a set of outcomes to which a probability is assigned. Typically, when the sample space is finite, any subset of the sample space is an _____. However, this approach does not work well in cases where the sample space is infinite, most notably when the outcome is a real number.
   a. Information set
   b. Equaliser
   c. Audio compression
   d. Event

2. In simple terms, two events are _____ if they cannot occur at the same time.

In logic, two _____ propositions are propositions that logically cannot both be true. To say that more than two propositions are _____ may, depending on context mean that no two of them can both be true, or only that they cannot all be true.

   a. Philosophy of mathematics
   b. Mutually exclusive
   c. Philosophy
   d. Determinism

3. _____ is the mathematical operation of scaling one number by another. It is one of the four basic operations in elementary arithmetic.

_____ is defined for whole numbers in terms of repeated addition; for example, 4 multiplied by 3 can be calculated by adding 3 copies of 4 together:

$$4 + 4 + 4 = 12.$$

_____ of rational numbers and real numbers is defined by systematic generalization of this basic idea.

   a. The number 0 is even.
   b. Highest common factor
   c. Least common multiple
   d. Multiplication

4. In mathematics, the _____ is a direct product of sets. The _____ is named after René Descartes, whose formulation of analytic geometry gave rise to this concept.

Specifically, the _____ of two sets X and Y, denoted X × Y, is the set of all possible ordered pairs whose first component is a member of X and whose second component is a member of Y:

$$X \times Y = \{(x,y) | x \in X \text{ and } y \in Y\}.$$

For example, the _____ of the 13-element set of standard playing card ranks {Ace, King, Queen, Jack, 10, 9, 8, 7, 6, 5, 4, 3, 2} and the four-element set of card suits {â™ , â™¥, â™¦, â™£} is the 52-element set of all possible playing cards ,, ...,,, ...,,}.

   a. Cartesian product
   b. Choice function
   c. Set of all sets
   d. Disjoint sets

5. In mathematics, a _____ is a convincing demonstration that some mathematical statement is necessarily true. _____s are obtained from deductive reasoning, rather than from inductive or empirical arguments. That is, a _____ must demonstrate that a statement is true in all cases, without a single exception.
   a. Congruent
   b. Germ
   c. Proof
   d. Conchoid

6. A _____ is a word, phrase, number or other sequence of units that can be read the same way in either direction. Composing literature in _____s is an example of constrained writing. The word '_____' was coined from Greek roots palin and dromos by English writer Ben Jonson in the 1600s.
   a. Metalanguage
   b. Palindrome
   c. 120-cell
   d. 1-center problem

7. In propositional logic, contraposition is a logical relationship between two statements of material implication. A proposition Q is materially implied by a proposition P when the following relationship holds:

$$(P \rightarrow Q)$$

In vernacular terms, this states 'If P then Q', or, 'If Socrates is a man then Socrates is human.' In a conditional such as this, P is called the antecedent and Q the consequent. One statement is the _____ of the other just when its antecedent is the negated consequent of the other, and vice-versa.

a. Continuous signal
b. Contour map
c. Contrapositive
d. Control chart

Chapter 7. Permutations and Combinations

1. In mathematics, the _____ of a non-negative integer n, denoted by n!, is the product of all positive integers less than or equal to n. For example,

$$5! = 1 \times 2 \times 3 \times 4 \times 5 = 120$$

and
$$6! = 1 \times 2 \times 3 \times 4 \times 5 \times 6 = 720$$

The notation n! was introduced by Christian Kramp in 1808.

The _____ function is formally defined by

$$n! = \prod_{k=1}^{n} k \qquad \forall n \in \mathbb{N}.$$

The above definition incorporates the instance

$$0! = 1$$

as an instance of the fact that the product of no numbers at all is 1.

   a. Plane partition
   b. Symbolic combinatorics
   c. Factorial
   d. Partition of a set

2. _____ is an abbreviation of the Latin phrase 'quod erat demonstrandum' which means literally, 'that which was to be demonstrated'. The phrase is written in its abbreviated form at the end of a mathematical proof or philosophical argument, to signify that the last statement deduced was the one to be demonstrated, so the proof is complete.

The phrase is a translation into Latin of the original Greek á½…περ á¼"δει δειξαι. (hoper edei deixai) which was used by many early mathematicians including Euclid and Archimedes.

   a. Q.E.D.
   b. Nonconstructive proof
   c. Direct proof
   d. Proofs from THE BOOK

3. In several fields of mathematics the term _____ is used with different but closely related meanings. They all relate to the notion of mapping the elements of a set to other elements of the same set, i.e., exchanging elements of a set.

Chapter 7. Permutations and Combinations

The general concept of _____ can be defined more formally in different contexts:

In combinatorics, a _____ is usually understood to be a sequence containing each element from a finite set once, and only once.

  a. Linearly independent
  b. Cyclic permutation
  c. Tensor product
  d. Permutation

4. In elementary algebra, a _____ is a polynomial with two terms: the sum of two monomials. It is the simplest kind of polynomial except for a monomial.

The _____ $a^2 - b^2$ can be factored as the product of two other _____s:

$a^2 - b^2$.

The product of a pair of linear _____s a x + b and c x + d is:

2 +x + bd.

A _____ raised to the nth power, represented as

n

can be expanded by means of the _____ theorem or, equivalently, using Pascal's triangle.

  a. Real structure
  b. Cylindrical algebraic decomposition
  c. Rational root theorem
  d. Binomial

5. In mathematics, the _____ $\binom{n}{k}$ is the coefficient of the x^k term in the polynomial expansion of the binomial power ^{n}.

In combinatorics, $\binom{n}{k}$ is interpreted as the number of k-element subsets of an n-element set, that is the number of ways that k things can be 'chosen' from a set of n things. Hence, $\binom{n}{k}$ is often read as 'n choose k' and called the choose function of n and k.

a. Symbolic combinatorics
b. Binomial coefficient
c. Rule of product
d. Dyson conjecture

6. In mathematics, a _____ is a constant multiplicative factor of a certain object. For example, in the expression $9x^2$, the _____ of x^2 is 9.

The object can be such things as a variable, a vector, a function, etc.

a. Fibonacci polynomials
b. Multivariate division algorithm
c. Stability radius
d. Coefficient

7. In combinatorial mathematics, a _____ is an un-ordered collection of distinct elements, usually of a prescribed size and taken from a given set. Given such a set S, a _____ of elements of S is just a subset of S, where as always forsets the order of the elements is not taken into account. Also, as always forsets, no elements can be repeated more than once in a _____; this is often referred to as a 'collection without repetition'.

a. Sparsity
b. Fill-in
c. Heawood number
d. Combination

8. In combinatorial mathematics, a _____ is a permutation in which none of the elements of the set appear in their original positions. That is, it is a bijection φ from a set S into itself with no fixed points: for all x in S, ≠ x. A frequent problem is to count the number of _____s as a function of the number of elements of the set, often with additional constraints; these numbers are called subfactorials and are a special case of the rencontres numbers.

a. Rencontres number
b. Random permutation
c. Subfactorial
d. Derangement

9. Leonardo of Pisa (c. 1170 - c. 1250), also known as Leonardo Pisano, Leonardo Bonacci, Leonardo _____, or, most commonly, simply _____, was an Italian mathematician, considered by some 'the most talented mathematician of the Middle Ages'.

a. Fibonacci
b. Harry Hinsley
c. Ralph C. Merkle
d. Guido Castelnuovo

10. A _____ is one of the basic shapes of geometry: a polygon with three corners or vertices and three sides or edges which are line segments. A _____ with vertices A, B, and C is denoted ABC.

In Euclidean geometry any three non-collinear points determine a unique _____ and a unique plane.

a. 1-center problem
b. Kepler triangle
c. Fuhrmann circle
d. Triangle

Chapter 8. Algorithms

1. _____ is a theoretical computer scientist and professor of computer science and molecular biology at the University of Southern California. He is known for being a co-inventor of the RSA cryptosystem in 1977, and of DNA computing. RSA is in widespread use in security applications, including https.

   a. Harold Hall 'Doc' Keen
   b. William Kingdon Clifford
   c. Johann Karl August Radon
   d. Leonard Max Adleman

2. In mathematics, computing, linguistics and related subjects, an _____ is a sequence of finite instructions, often used for calculation and data processing. It is formally a type of effective method in which a list of well-defined instructions for completing a task will, when given an initial state, proceed through a well-defined series of successive states, eventually terminating in an end-state. The transition from one state to the next is not necessarily deterministic; some _____s, known as probabilistic _____s, incorporate randomness.

   a. In-place algorithm
   b. Out-of-core
   c. Approximate counting algorithm
   d. Algorithm

3. _____ is the mathematical operation of scaling one number by another. It is one of the four basic operations in elementary arithmetic.

   _____ is defined for whole numbers in terms of repeated addition; for example, 4 multiplied by 3 can be calculated by adding 3 copies of 4 together:

   $$4 + 4 + 4 = 12.$$

   _____ of rational numbers and real numbers is defined by systematic generalization of this basic idea.

   a. The number 0 is even.
   b. Highest common factor
   c. Least common multiple
   d. Multiplication

4. _____ is a systematic method for multiplying two numbers that does not require the multiplication table, only the ability to multiply and divide by 2, and to add. Also known as Egyptian multiplication and Peasant multiplication, it decomposes one of the multiplicands into a sum of powers of two and creates a table of doublings of the second multiplicand. This method may be called mediation and duplation, where mediation means halving one number and duplation means doubling the other number.

Chapter 8. Algorithms

a. A Mathematical Theory of Communication
b. A posteriori
c. A chemical equation
d. Ancient Egyptian multiplication

5. In graph theory, a _____ is an edge that connects a vertex to itself. A simple graph contains no _____s.

Depending on the context, a graph or a multigraph may be defined so as to either allow or disallow the presence of _____s:

- Where graphs are defined so as to allow _____s and multiple edges, a graph without _____s is often called a multigraph.
- Where graphs are defined so as to disallow _____s and multiple edges, a multigraph or a pseudograph is often defined to mean a 'graph' which can have _____s and multiple edges.

For an undirected graph, the degree of a vertex is equal to the number of adjacent vertices.

A special case is a _____, which adds two to the degree.

a. Commensurable
b. Loop
c. FISH
d. Duality

6. In general usage, _____ often tends to be used to characterize something with many parts in intricate arrangement. In science there are at this time a number of approaches to characterizing _____, many of which are reflected in Seth Lloyd of M.I.T. writes that he once gave a presentation which set out 32 definitions of _____.

Definitions are often tied to the concept of a 'system' - a set of parts or elements which have relationships among them differentiated from relationships with other elements outside the relational regime.

a. 2-3 heap
b. 1-center problem
c. 120-cell
d. Complexity

7. The mathematical concept of a _____ expresses the intuitive idea of deterministic dependence between two quantities, one of which is viewed as primary and the other as secondary. A _____ then is a way to associate a unique output for each input of a specified type, for example, a real number or an element of a given set.

a. Grill
b. Coherent
c. Going up
d. Function

8. In computational complexity theory, the complexity class _____ is a class of problems having two properties:

 - Any given solution to the problem can be verified quickly; the set of problems with this property is called NP.
 - If the problem can be solved quickly, then so can every problem in NP.

Although any given solution to such a problem can be verified quickly, there is no known efficient way to locate a solution in the first place; indeed, the most notable characteristic of _____ problems is that no fast solution to them is known. That is, the time required to solve the problem using any currently known algorithm increases very quickly as the size of the problem grows. As a result, the time required to solve even moderately large versions of many of these problems easily reaches into the billions or trillions of years, using any amount of computing power available today. As a consequence, determining whether or not it is possible to solve these problems quickly is one of the principal unsolved problems in computer science today.

a. Quadratic assignment problem
b. NP-complete
c. 3-partition problem
d. Subset sum

9. In mathematics, an _____ is a statement about the relative size or order of two objects, or about whether they are the same or not

 - The notation $a < b$ means that a is less than b.
 - The notation $a > b$ means that a is greater than b.
 - The notation $a \neq b$ means that a is not equal to b, but does not say that one is bigger than the other or even that they can be compared in size.

In all these cases, a is not equal to b, hence, '_____'.

These relations are known as strict _____

 - The notation $a \leq b$ means that a is less than or equal to b;
 - The notation $a \geq b$ means that a is greater than or equal to b;

An additional use of the notation is to show that one quantity is much greater than another, normally by several orders of magnitude.

- The notation a << b means that a is much less than b.
- The notation a >> b means that a is much greater than b.

If the sense of the _____ is the same for all values of the variables for which its members are defined, then the _____ is called an 'absolute' or 'unconditional' _____. If the sense of an _____ holds only for certain values of the variables involved, but is reversed or destroyed for other values of the variables, it is called a conditional _____.

An _____ may appear unsolvable because it only states whether a number is larger or smaller than another number; but it is possible to apply the same operations for equalities to inequalities. For example, to find x for the _____ 10x > 23 one would divide 23 by 10.

   a. A chemical equation
   b. Inequality
   c. A Mathematical Theory of Communication
   d. A posteriori

10. In mathematics, a _____ is a convincing demonstration that some mathematical statement is necessarily true. _____s are obtained from deductive reasoning, rather than from inductive or empirical arguments. That is, a _____ must demonstrate that a statement is true in all cases, without a single exception.
   a. Congruent
   b. Proof
   c. Conchoid
   d. Germ

11. In geometry, a _____ is a convex regular polyhedron. These are the three-dimensional analogs of the convex regular polygons. There are precisely five such figures.
   a. 1-center problem
   b. 120-cell
   c. Platonic solid
   d. 2-3 heap

12. _____ is an abbreviation of the Latin phrase 'quod erat demonstrandum' which means literally, 'that which was to be demonstrated'. The phrase is written in its abbreviated form at the end of a mathematical proof or philosophical argument, to signify that the last statement deduced was the one to be demonstrated, so the proof is complete.

The phrase is a translation into Latin of the original Greek ἅ½...περ á¼"δει δειξαι. (hoper edei deixai) which was used by many early mathematicians including Euclid and Archimedes.

a. Q.E.D.
b. Nonconstructive proof
c. Proofs from THE BOOK
d. Direct proof

13. In complexity theory, _____ is the computation time of a problem where the time to complete the computation, m

Written mathematically, there exists k > 1 such that m

a. Asymptotic time complexity
b. Element uniqueness
c. Optimal solution
d. Exponential time

14. In mathematics, a _____ is an expression constructed from variables and constants, using the operations of addition, subtraction, multiplication, and constant non-negative whole number exponents. For example, $x^2 - 4x + 7$ is a _____, but $x^2 - 4/x + 7x^{3/2}$ is not, because its second term involves division by the variable x and also because its third term contains an exponent that is not a whole number.

_____s are one of the most important concepts in algebra and throughout mathematics and science.

a. Group extension
b. Polynomial
c. Coimage
d. Semifield

15. In computational complexity theory, _____ refers to the computation time of a problem where the run time, m, is no greater than a polynomial function of the problem size, n.

Written mathematically using big O notation, this states that m for some natural number k. For example, the quicksort sorting algorithm on n integers performs at most An^2 operations for some constant A.

a. Polynomial-time reduction
b. Generalized game
c. Linearithmic
d. Polynomial time

16. In computational complexity theory, an algorithm is said to take _____ if the asymptotic upper bound for the time it requires is proportional to the size of the input, which is usually denoted n.

Informally spoken, the running time increases linearly with the size of the input. For example, a procedure that adds up all elements of a list requires time proportional to the length of the list.

a. Truth table reduction
b. Linear time
c. Time-constructible function
d. Constructible function

17. In number theory, the _____ is an algorithm to determine the greatest common divisor of two elements of any Euclidean domain. Its major significance is that it does not require factoring the two integers, and it is also significant in that it is one of the oldest algorithms known, dating back to the ancient Greeks.

The _____ is one of the oldest algorithms known, since it appeared in Euclid's Elements around 300 BC.

a. A Mathematical Theory of Communication
b. Euclidean algorithm
c. A posteriori
d. A chemical equation

18. Leonardo of Pisa (c. 1170 - c. 1250), also known as Leonardo Pisano, Leonardo Bonacci, Leonardo _____, or, most commonly, simply _____, was an Italian mathematician, considered by some 'the most talented mathematician of the Middle Ages'.
a. Ralph C. Merkle
b. Fibonacci
c. Harry Hinsley
d. Guido Castelnuovo

19. In mathematics, a _____ is a statement that can be proved on the basis of explicitly stated or previously agreed assumptions.

Chapter 8. Algorithms

a. Boolean function
b. Logical value
c. Disjunction introduction
d. Theorem

20. In computer science, _____ is a search algorithm that is suitable for searching a list of data for a particular value.

It operates by checking every element of a list one at a time in sequence until a match is found. _____ runs in .

a. Perfect hash function
b. Linear hashing
c. Linear probing
d. Linear search

21. A _____ algorithm is a technique for locating a particular value in a sorted list of values. To cast this in the frame of the guessing game, realize that we seek to guess the index, or numbered place, of the value in the list. The method makes progressively better guesses, and closes in on the location of the sought value by selecting the middle element in the span, comparing its value to the target value, and determining if the selected value is greater than, less than, or equal to the target value.
a. Binary search
b. 1-center problem
c. 120-cell
d. 2-3 heap

22. _____ is a simple sorting algorithm. It works by repeatedly stepping through the list to be sorted, comparing two items at a time and swapping them if they are in the wrong order. The pass through the list is repeated until no swaps are needed, which indicates that the list is sorted.
a. Pseudo-code
b. Bubble sort
c. 120-cell
d. 1-center problem

23. _____ was a mathematician of great scope and depth.

He was the son of the famous economist Carl Menger.

He worked in mathematics on algebras, curve and dimension theory, and geometries.

a. Gustave Bertrand
b. Karl Menger
c. Solomon Lefschetz
d. Frederick William Winterbotham

24. In quantum field theory and statistical mechanics in the thermodynamic limit, a system with a global symmetry can have more than one phase. For parameters where the symmetry is spontaneously broken, the system is said to be _____. When the global symmetry is unbroken the system is disordered.
   a. Einstein relation
   b. Isoenthalpic-isobaric ensemble
   c. Ursell function
   d. Ordered

25. In computer science, _____ or merge_sort is an O
   a. 2-3 heap
   b. 120-cell
   c. 1-center problem
   d. Merge sort

26. A _____ is a piece of cloth, often flown from a pole or mast, generally used symbolically for signaling or identification. The term _____ is also used to refer to the graphic design employed by a _____, or to its depiction in another medium.

The first _____s were used to assist military coordination on battlefields, and _____s have since evolved into a general tool for rudimentary signaling and identification, it was especially used in environments where communication is similarly challenging (such as the maritime environment where semaphore is used.)

   a. 1-center problem
   b. Flag
   c. 2-3 heap
   d. 120-cell

27. _____ or trinary is the base-3 numeral system. Analogous to a 'bit', a _____ digit is known as a trit (trinary digit.) One trit contains about 1.58596 ($\log_2 3$) bit of information.

Chapter 8. Algorithms

a. Ternary
b. Radix
c. Negafibonacci
d. Decimal point

28. A _____ algorithm is a computer science technique for finding the minimum or maximum of a function that is either strictly increasing and then strictly decreasing or vice versa. A _____ determines either that the minimum or maximum cannot be in the first third of the domain or that it cannot be in the last third of the domain, then repeats on the remaining two-thirds. A _____ is an example of a divide and conquer algorithm.

a. Horspool
b. Brute-force search
c. Ternary search
d. Locality sensitive hashing

29. In mathematics, an _____ in the sense of ring theory is a subring $\mathcal{O}$ of a ring R that satisfies the conditions

1. R is a ring which is a finite-dimensional algebra over the rational number field $\mathbb{Q}$
2. $\mathcal{O}$ spans R over $\mathbb{Q}$, so that $\mathbb{Q}\mathcal{O} = R$, and
3. $\mathcal{O}$ is a lattice in R.

The third condition can be stated more accurately, in terms of the extension of scalars of R to the real numbers, embedding R in a real vector space. In less formal terms, additively $\mathcal{O}$ should be a free abelian group generated by a basis for R over $\mathbb{Q}$.

The leading example is the case where R is a number field K and $\mathcal{O}$ is its ring of integers. In algebraic number theory there are examples for any K other than the rational field of proper subrings of the ring of integers that are also _____ s.

a. Annihilator
b. Efficiency
c. Algebraic
d. Order

30. In several fields of mathematics the term _____ is used with different but closely related meanings. They all relate to the notion of mapping the elements of a set to other elements of the same set, i.e., exchanging elements of a set.

The general concept of _____ can be defined more formally in different contexts:

In combinatorics, a _____ is usually understood to be a sequence containing each element from a finite set once, and only once.

a. Linearly independent
b. Cyclic permutation
c. Tensor product
d. Permutation

31. In combinatorial mathematics, a _____ is an un-ordered collection of distinct elements, usually of a prescribed size and taken from a given set. Given such a set S, a _____ of elements of S is just a subset of S, where as always forsets the order of the elements is not taken into account. Also, as always forsets, no elements can be repeated more than once in a _____; this is often referred to as a 'collection without repetition'.

a. Sparsity
b. Fill-in
c. Combination
d. Heawood number

Chapter 9. Graphs

1. A _____ is a structure built to span a gorge, valley, road, railroad track, river, body of water for the purpose of providing passage over the obstacle. Designs of _____s will vary depending on the function of the _____ and the nature of the terrain where the _____ is to be constructed. Roman _____ of Córdoba, Spain, built in the 1st century BC. Ponte di Pietra in Verona, Italy. A log _____ in the French Alps near Vallorcine. An English 18th century example of a _____ in the Palladian style, with shops on the span: Pulteney _____, Bath A Han Dynasty Chinese miniature model of two residential towers joined by a _____

The first _____s were made by nature -- as simple as a log fallen across a stream.

   a. 120-cell
   b. 2-3 heap
   c. Bridge
   d. 1-center problem

2. The '_____' puzzle consists of four cubes with faces colored with four colors. The object of the puzzle is to stack these cubes in a column so that each side of the stack shows each of the four colors. The distribution of colors on each cube is unique.
   a. Eulerian path
   b. Independent set
   c. Induced path
   d. Instant Insanity

3. The _____ is a unique, numerical commercial book identifier, based upon the 9-digit Standard Book Numbering code created in the UK by the booksellers and stationers W.H. Smith and others in 1966. The 10-digit _____ format was developed by the International Organization for Standardization and published as an international standard, ISO 2108, in 1970. Currently, the ISO TC 46/SC 9 is responsible for the standard.
   a. A Mathematical Theory of Communication
   b. ISBN
   c. A posteriori
   d. A chemical equation

4. _____ or set diagrams are diagrams that show all hypothetically possible logical relations between a finite collection of sets. _____ were invented around 1880 by John Venn. They are used in many fields, including set theory, probability, logic, statistics, and computer science.
   a. 2-3 heap
   b. 1-center problem
   c. 120-cell
   d. Venn diagrams

5. _____ is an adjective meaning contiguous, adjoining or abutting.

In geometry, _____ is when sides meet to make an angle.

In trigonometry the _____ side of a right angled triangle is the cathetus next to the angle in question.

   a. Ordered geometry
   b. Affine geometry
   c. Ambient space
   d. Adjacent

6. A _____ is a 2D geometric symbolic representation of information according to some visualization technique. Sometimes, the technique uses a 3D visualization which is then projected onto the 2D surface. The word graph is sometimes used as a synonym for _____.
   a. 120-cell
   b. 2-3 heap
   c. 1-center problem
   d. Diagram

7. In graph theory, a _____ is an edge that connects a vertex to itself. A simple graph contains no _____s.

Depending on the context, a graph or a multigraph may be defined so as to either allow or disallow the presence of _____s:

   • Where graphs are defined so as to allow _____s and multiple edges, a graph without _____s is often called a multigraph.
   • Where graphs are defined so as to disallow _____s and multiple edges, a multigraph or a pseudograph is often defined to mean a 'graph' which can have _____s and multiple edges.

For an undirected graph, the degree of a vertex is equal to the number of adjacent vertices.

A special case is a _____, which adds two to the degree.

   a. FISH
   b. Commensurable
   c. Duality
   d. Loop

8. In geometry, a _____ is a special kind of point, usually a corner of a polygon, polyhedron, or higher dimensional polytope. In the geometry of curves a _____ is a point of where the first derivative of curvature is zero. In graph theory, a _____ is the fundamental unit out of which graphs are formed
   a. Crib
   b. Dini
   c. Duality
   d. Vertex

9. _____ is a method of mathematical proof typically used to establish that a given statement is true of all natural numbers. It is done by proving that the first statement in the infinite sequence of statements is true, and then proving that if any one statement in the infinite sequence of statements is true, then so is the next one.

The method can be extended to prove statements about more general well-founded structures, such as trees; this generalization, known as structural induction, is used in mathematical logic and computer science.

   a. Herbrand structure
   b. Ground expression
   c. Mathematical Induction
   d. Finitary

10. In mathematical analysis, a metric space M is said to be _____ (or Cauchy) if every Cauchy sequence of points in M has a limit that is also in M or alternatively if every Cauchy sequence in M converges in M.

Intuitively, a space is _____ if there are no 'points missing' from it (inside or at the boundary.) For instance, the set of rational numbers is not _____, because $\sqrt{2}$ is 'missing' from it, even though one can construct a Cauchy sequence of rational numbers that converges to it.

   a. 2-3 heap
   b. 120-cell
   c. 1-center problem
   d. Complete

11. A _____ is one of the basic shapes of geometry: a polygon with three corners or vertices and three sides or edges which are line segments. A _____ with vertices A, B, and C is denoted ABC.

In Euclidean geometry any three non-collinear points determine a unique _____ and a unique plane.

a. Kepler triangle
b. 1-center problem
c. Fuhrmann circle
d. Triangle

12. In mathematics, a _____ is a statement that can be proved on the basis of explicitly stated or previously agreed assumptions.
    a. Boolean function
    b. Disjunction introduction
    c. Theorem
    d. Logical value

13. In category theory, two categories C and D are _____ if there exist functors F : C → D and G : D → C which are mutually inverse to each other. This means that both the objects and the morphisms of C and D stand in a one to one correspondence to each other. Two _____ categories share all properties that are defined solely in terms of category theory; for all practical purposes, they are identical and differ only in the notation of their objects and morphisms.
    a. Automorphism group
    b. Epimorphism
    c. Isomorphic
    d. Isomorphism

14. In abstract algebra, an _____ is a bijective map f such that both f and its inverse f^{-1} are homomorphisms.

In the more general setting of category theory, an _____ is a morphism f:X→Y in a category for which there exists an 'inverse' f^{-1}:Y→X, with the property that both $f^{-1}f=id_X$ and $ff^{-1}=id_Y$.

Informally, an _____ is a kind of mapping between objects, which shows a relationship between two properties or operations.

   a. Epimorphism
   b. Automorphism group
   c. Isomorphic
   d. Isomorphism

15. In functional analysis, a Banach space is called _____ if it satisfies a certain abstract property involving dual spaces. _____ spaces turn out to have desirable geometric properties.

Suppose X is a normed vector space over R or C.

a. Reflexive
b. Copula
c. Boolean algebra
d. Gamma test

16. _____ is an abbreviation of the Latin phrase 'quod erat demonstrandum' which means literally, 'that which was to be demonstrated'. The phrase is written in its abbreviated form at the end of a mathematical proof or philosophical argument, to signify that the last statement deduced was the one to be demonstrated, so the proof is complete.

The phrase is a translation into Latin of the original Greek á½…περ á¼"δει δειξαι. (hoper edei deixai) which was used by many early mathematicians including Euclid and Archimedes.

a. Nonconstructive proof
b. Direct proof
c. Proofs from THE BOOK
d. Q.E.D.

17. In geometry, a _____ is a polygon with four sides or edges and four vertices or corners. Sometimes, the term quadrangle is used, for etymological symmetry with triangle, and sometimes tetragon for consistency with pentagon, hexagon and so on. The interior angles of a _____ add up to 360 degrees of arc.

a. 120-cell
b. 1-center problem
c. 2-3 heap
d. Quadrilateral

1. In computational complexity theory, the complexity class _____ is a class of problems having two properties:

   - Any given solution to the problem can be verified quickly; the set of problems with this property is called NP.
   - If the problem can be solved quickly, then so can every problem in NP.

Although any given solution to such a problem can be verified quickly, there is no known efficient way to locate a solution in the first place; indeed, the most notable characteristic of _____ problems is that no fast solution to them is known. That is, the time required to solve the problem using any currently known algorithm increases very quickly as the size of the problem grows. As a result, the time required to solve even moderately large versions of many of these problems easily reaches into the billions or trillions of years, using any amount of computing power available today. As a consequence, determining whether or not it is possible to solve these problems quickly is one of the principal unsolved problems in computer science today.

   a. Subset sum
   b. 3-partition problem
   c. Quadratic assignment problem
   d. NP-complete

2. In mathematics, a _____ is a statement that can be proved on the basis of explicitly stated or previously agreed assumptions.
   a. Logical value
   b. Disjunction introduction
   c. Boolean function
   d. Theorem

3. The Tower of Hanoi or _____ is a mathematical game or puzzle. It consists of three rods, and a number of disks of different sizes which can slide onto any rod. The puzzle starts with the disks neatly stacked in order of size on one rod, the smallest at the top, thus making a conical shape.
   a. 2-3 heap
   b. Towers of Hanoi
   c. 1-center problem
   d. 120-cell

4. In graph theory, a _____ in a graph is a sequence of vertices such that from each of its vertices there is an edge to the next vertex in the sequence. The first vertex is called the start vertex and the last vertex is called the end vertex. Both of them are called end or terminal vertices of the _____.

a. Path
b. Class
c. Deltoid
d. Blinding

5. Walking is the main form of animal locomotion on land, distinguished from running and crawling. When carried out in shallow waters, it is usually described as wading and when performed over a steeply rising object or an obstacle it becomes scrambling or climbing. The word _____ is descended from the Old English wealcan 'to roll'.

a. Walk
b. 120-cell
c. 1-center problem
d. 2-3 heap

6. _____, in logic and fields that rely on it such as mathematics and philosophy, is a biconditional logical connective between statements. In that it is biconditional, the connective can be likened to the standard material conditional ('if') combined with its reverse ('only if'); hence the name. The result is that the truth of either one of the connected statements requires the truth of the other.

a. If and only if
b. Algebraic logic
c. Existential graph
d. Enumerative definition

7. _____ is a method of mathematical proof typically used to establish that a given statement is true of all natural numbers. It is done by proving that the first statement in the infinite sequence of statements is true, and then proving that if any one statement in the infinite sequence of statements is true, then so is the next one.

The method can be extended to prove statements about more general well-founded structures, such as trees; this generalization, known as structural induction, is used in mathematical logic and computer science.

a. Herbrand structure
b. Ground expression
c. Finitary
d. Mathematical Induction

8. In mathematics, a _____ is a convincing demonstration that some mathematical statement is necessarily true. _____s are obtained from deductive reasoning, rather than from inductive or empirical arguments. That is, a _____ must demonstrate that a statement is true in all cases, without a single exception.

a. Congruent
b. Germ
c. Conchoid
d. Proof

9. _____ reductio ad impossibile is a type of logical argument where one assumes a claim for the sake of argument and derives an absurd or ridiculous outcome, and then concludes that the original claim must have been wrong as it led to an absurd result.

It makes use of the law of non-contradiction -- a statement cannot be both true and false. In some cases it may also make use of the law of excluded middle -- a statement must be either true or false.

a. Reductio ad absurdum
b. 1-center problem
c. 2-3 heap
d. 120-cell

10. _____ is an abbreviation of the Latin phrase 'quod erat demonstrandum' which means literally, 'that which was to be demonstrated'. The phrase is written in its abbreviated form at the end of a mathematical proof or philosophical argument, to signify that the last statement deduced was the one to be demonstrated, so the proof is complete.

The phrase is a translation into Latin of the original Greek á½...περ á¼"δει δειξαι. (hoper edei deixai) which was used by many early mathematicians including Euclid and Archimedes.

a. Direct proof
b. Nonconstructive proof
c. Proofs from THE BOOK
d. Q.E.D.

11. _____, in mathematics, are a non-commutative extension of complex numbers. They were first described by the Irish mathematician Sir William Rowan Hamilton in 1843 and applied to mechanics in three-dimensional space. They find uses in both theoretical and applied mathematics, in particular for calculations involving three-dimensional rotations, such as in 3D computer graphics, although they have been superseded in many applications by vectors and matrices.
a. Split-biquaternion
b. Generalized quaternion interpolation
c. Hurwitz quaternion
d. Quaternions

Chapter 10. Paths and Circuits

12. A _____ is any polyhedron with twelve faces, but usually a regular _____ is meant: a Platonic solid composed of twelve regular pentagonal faces, with three meeting at each vertex. It has twenty vertices and thirty edges. Its dual polyhedron is the icosahedron.
    a. 120-cell
    b. 2-3 heap
    c. 1-center problem
    d. Dodecahedron

13. In geometry, a _____ is a convex regular polyhedron. These are the three-dimensional analogs of the convex regular polygons. There are precisely five such figures.
    a. 2-3 heap
    b. 1-center problem
    c. 120-cell
    d. Platonic solid

14. In geometry, an _____ is any polyhedron having 20 faces, but usually a regular _____ is implied, which has equilateral triangles as faces.

    The regular _____ is one of the five Platonic solids. It is a convex regular polyhedron composed of twenty triangular faces, with five meeting at each of the twelve vertices.

    a. Icosahedron
    b. A Mathematical Theory of Communication
    c. A posteriori
    d. A chemical equation

15. In mathematics and computer science, the _____ of a finite directed or undirected graph G on n vertices is the n × n matrix where the nondiagonal entry a_{ij} is the number of edges from vertex i to vertex j, and the diagonal entry a_{ii} is either twice the number of loops at vertex i or just the number of loops. There exists a unique _____ for each graph, and it is not the _____ of any other graph. In the special case of a finite simple graph, the _____ is a-matrix with zeros on its diagonal.
    a. A posteriori
    b. A Mathematical Theory of Communication
    c. A chemical equation
    d. Adjacency matrix

16. In mathematics, a _____ is a rectangular table of elements, which may be numbers or, more generally, any abstract quantities that can be added and multiplied. Matrices are used to describe linear equations, keep track of the coefficients of linear transformations and to record data that depend on multiple parameters. Matrices are described by the field of _____ theory.
   a. Double counting
   b. Coherent
   c. Compression
   d. Matrix

17. In mathematics, the term _____ has several different important meanings:

   - An _____ is an equality that remains true regardless of the values of any variables that appear within it, to distinguish it from an equality which is true under more particular conditions. For this, the 'triple bar' symbol ≡ is sometimes used.
   - In algebra, an _____ or _____ element of a set S with a binary operation Â· is an element e that, when combined with any element x of S, produces that same x. That is, eÂ·x = xÂ·e = x for all x in S.
     o The _____ function from a set S to itself, often denoted id or id_S, s the function such that i = x for all x in S. This function serves as the _____ element in the set of all functions from S to itself with respect to function composition.
     o In linear algebra, the _____ matrix of size n is the n-by-n square matrix with ones on the main diagonal and zeros elsewhere. This matrix serves as the _____ with respect to matrix multiplication.

A common example of the first meaning is the trigonometric _____

$$\sin^2 \theta + \cos^2 \theta = 1$$

which is true for all real values of θ, as opposed to

$$\cos \theta = 1,$$

which is true only for some values of θ, not all. For example, the latter equation is true when $\theta = 0$, false when $\theta = 2$

Chapter 10. Paths and Circuits

The concepts of 'additive _____' and 'multiplicative _____' are central to the Peano axioms. The number 0 is the 'additive _____' for integers, real numbers, and complex numbers. For the real numbers, for all $a \in \mathbb{R}$,

$$0 + a = a,$$

$$a + 0 = a, \text{ and}$$

$$0 + 0 = 0.$$

Similarly, The number 1 is the 'multiplicative _____' for integers, real numbers, and complex numbers.

a. ARIA
b. Intersection
c. Action
d. Identity

18. In several fields of mathematics the term _____ is used with different but closely related meanings. They all relate to the notion of mapping the elements of a set to other elements of the same set, i.e., exchanging elements of a set.

The general concept of _____ can be defined more formally in different contexts:

In combinatorics, a _____ is usually understood to be a sequence containing each element from a finite set once, and only once.

a. Permutation
b. Tensor product
c. Cyclic permutation
d. Linearly independent

19. In linear algebra, the _____ of a matrix A is another matrix A^T created by any one of the following equivalent actions:

- write the rows of A as the columns of A^T
- write the columns of A as the rows of A^T
- reflect A by its main diagonal to obtain A^T

Formally, the _____ of an m × n matrix A is the n × m matrix

$$\mathbf{A}^T_{ij} = \mathbf{A}_{ji} \text{ for } 1 \leq i \leq n, 1 \leq j \leq m.$$

- $\begin{bmatrix} 1 & 2 \\ 3 & 4 \end{bmatrix}^T = \begin{bmatrix} 1 & 3 \\ 2 & 4 \end{bmatrix}.$

- $\begin{bmatrix} 1 & 2 \\ 3 & 4 \\ 5 & 6 \end{bmatrix}^T = \begin{bmatrix} 1 & 3 & 5 \\ 2 & 4 & 6 \end{bmatrix}.$

For matrices A, B and scalar c we have the following properties of _____:

1. $\left(\mathbf{A}^T\right)^T = \mathbf{A}$

    Taking the _____ is an involution.

- $(\mathbf{A} + \mathbf{B})^T = \mathbf{A}^T + \mathbf{B}^T$

    The _____ respects addition.

- $(\mathbf{AB})^T = \mathbf{B}^T\mathbf{A}^T$

    Note that the order of the factors reverses. From this one can deduce that a square matrix A is invertible if and only if A^T is invertible, and in this case we have $^T = ^{-1}$. It is relatively easy to extend this result to the general case of multiple matrices, where we find that $^T = Z^T Y^T X^T ... C^T B^T A^T$.

- $(c\mathbf{A})^T = c\mathbf{A}^T$

    The _____ of a scalar is the same scalar. Together with, this states that the _____ is a linear map from the space of m × n matrices to the space of all n × m matrices.

- $\det(\mathbf{A}^T) = \det(\mathbf{A})$

    The determinant of a matrix is the same as that of its _____.

- The dot product of two column vectors a and b can be computed as

$$\mathbf{a} \cdot \mathbf{b} = \mathbf{a}^\mathrm{T} \mathbf{b},$$

which is written as $a_i\, b^i$ in Einstein notation.
- If A has only real entries, then $A^\mathrm{T}A$ is a positive-semidefinite matrix.
- $(\mathbf{A}^\mathrm{T})^{-1} = (\mathbf{A}^{-1})^\mathrm{T}$

   The _____ of an invertible matrix is also invertible, and its inverse is the _____ of the inverse of the original matrix.

- If A is a square matrix, then its eigenvalues are equal to the eigenvalues of its _____.

A square matrix whose _____ is equal to itself is called a symmetric matrix; that is, A is symmetric if

$$\mathbf{A}^\mathrm{T} = \mathbf{A}.$$

A square matrix whose _____ is also its inverse is called an orthogonal matrix; that is, G is orthogonal if

$$\mathbf{G}\mathbf{G}^\mathrm{T} = \mathbf{G}^\mathrm{T}\mathbf{G} = \mathbf{I}_n,$$ the identity matrix.

A square matrix whose _____ is equal to its negative is called skew-symmetric matrix; that is, A is skew-symmetric if

$$\mathbf{A}^\mathrm{T} = -\mathbf{A}.$$

The conjugate _____ of the complex matrix A, written as A^*, is obtained by taking the _____ of A and the complex conjugate of each entry:

$$\mathbf{A}^* = (\overline{\mathbf{A}})^\mathrm{T} = \overline{(\mathbf{A}^\mathrm{T})}.$$

If f: V→W is a linear map between vector spaces V and W with nondegenerate bilinear forms, we define the _____ of f to be the linear map ${}^t f$: W→V, determined by

$$B_V(v, {}^t f(w)) = B_W(f(v), w) \quad \forall\, v \in V, w \in W.$$

Here, B_V and B_W are the bilinear forms on V and W respectively. The matrix of the _____ of a map is the transposed matrix only if the bases are orthonormal with respect to their bilinear forms.

Over a complex vector space, one often works with sesquilinear forms instead of bilinear.

a. Transpose
b. Tridiagonal matrix
c. Cartan matrix
d. Polynomial matrix

20. In graph theory, the _____ problem is the problem of finding a path between two vertices such that the sum of the weights of its constituent edges is minimized. An example is finding the quickest way to get from one location to another on a road map; in this case, the vertices represent locations and the edges represent segments of road and are weighted by the time needed to travel that segment.

Formally, given a weighted graph, and one element v of V, find a path P from v to each v' of V so that

$$\sum_{p \in P} f(p)$$

is minimal among all paths connecting v to v'.

a. Shortest path
b. Hamiltonian path
c. Random graph
d. Bottleneck traveling salesman problem

21. In the physical sciences, _____ is a measurement of the gravitational force acting on an object. Near the surface of the Earth, the acceleration due to gravity is approximately constant; this means that an object's _____ is roughly proportional to its mass.

In commerce and in many other applications, _____ means the same as mass as that term is used in physics.

a. 1-center problem
b. Weight
c. 120-cell
d. 2-3 heap

22. In mathematics, computing, linguistics and related subjects, an _____ is a sequence of finite instructions, often used for calculation and data processing. It is formally a type of effective method in which a list of well-defined instructions for completing a task will, when given an initial state, proceed through a well-defined series of successive states, eventually terminating in an end-state. The transition from one state to the next is not necessarily deterministic; some _____s, known as probabilistic _____s, incorporate randomness.

a. Algorithm
b. In-place algorithm
c. Approximate counting algorithm
d. Out-of-core

23. In general usage, _____ often tends to be used to characterize something with many parts in intricate arrangement. In science there are at this time a number of approaches to characterizing _____, many of which are reflected in Seth Lloyd of M.I.T. writes that he once gave a presentation which set out 32 definitions of _____.

Definitions are often tied to the concept of a 'system' - a set of parts or elements which have relationships among them differentiated from relationships with other elements outside the relational regime.

a. 120-cell
b. 2-3 heap
c. 1-center problem
d. Complexity

24. In computer science, the _____ is a graph analysis algorithm for finding shortest paths in a weighted, directed graph. A single execution of the algorithm will find the shortest paths between all pairs of vertices. The _____ is an example of dynamic programming.
a. Breadth-first search
b. Depth-limited search
c. Floyd-Warshall algorithm
d. Topological sorting

Chapter 11. Applications of Paths and Circuits

1. In graph theory, a branch of mathematics, the _____, postman tour or route inspection problem is to find a shortest closed trail that visits every edge of a undirected graph. When the graph has an Eulerian circuit, that circuit is an optimal solution.

Alan Goldman of NIST first coined the name '_____' for this problem, as it was originally studied by the Chinese mathematician Mei-Ku Kuan in 1962.

   a. Bipartite dimension
   b. Bottleneck traveling salesman
   c. Liquid schedule
   d. Chinese Postman Problem

2. Leonardo of Pisa (c. 1170 - c. 1250), also known as Leonardo Pisano, Leonardo Bonacci, Leonardo _____, or, most commonly, simply _____, was an Italian mathematician, considered by some 'the most talented mathematician of the Middle Ages'.
   a. Harry Hinsley
   b. Guido Castelnuovo
   c. Ralph C. Merkle
   d. Fibonacci

3. In mathematics, a _____ is a statement that can be proved on the basis of explicitly stated or previously agreed assumptions.
   a. Logical value
   b. Boolean function
   c. Disjunction introduction
   d. Theorem

4. In mathematics and computer science, _____ (also base-16, hexa or base, of 16. It uses sixteen distinct symbols, most often the symbols 0-9 to represent values zero to nine, and A, B, C, D, E, F (or a through f) to represent values ten to fifteen.

Its primary use is as a human friendly representation of binary coded values, so it is often used in digital electronics and computer engineering.

   a. Hexadecimal
   b. Radix
   c. Factoradic
   d. Tetradecimal

5. In statistics, the _____ or _____ function is the partial derivative, with respect to some parameter θ, of the logarithm of the likelihood function. If the observation is X and its likelihood is L, then the _____ V can be found through the chain rule:

$$V = \frac{\partial}{\partial \theta} \log L(\theta; X) = \frac{1}{L(\theta; X)} \frac{\partial L(\theta; X)}{\partial \theta}.$$

Note that V is a function of θ and the observation X, so that, in general, it is not a statistic. Note also that V indicates the sensitivity of L.

a. Score
b. Cleaver
c. Deviation
d. Functional

6. A _____ is a competition involving a relatively large number of competitors, all participating in a sport or game. More specifically, the term may be used in either of two overlapping senses:

   1. One or more competitions held at a single venue and concentrated into a relatively short time interval. Some game clubs focus on preparing members for such _____s. Chess clubs, for instance, frequently employ similar ranking systems, chess clocks, and etiquette to those used in chess _____s.
   2. A competition involving multiple matches, each involving a subset of the competitors, with the overall _____ winner determined based on the combined results of these individual matches. These are common in those sports and games where each match must involve a small number of competitors: often precisely two, as in most team sports, racket sports and combat sports, many card games and board games, and many forms of competitive debating. Such _____s allow large numbers to compete against each other in spite of the restriction on numbers in a single match.

These two senses are distinct. All golf _____s meet the first definition, but while match play _____s meet the second, stroke play _____s do not, since there are no distinct matches within the _____. In contrast, football leagues like the Premier League are _____s in the second sense, but not the first, having matches spread across many stadia over a period of up to a year.

a. 120-cell
b. Tournament
c. 2-3 heap
d. 1-center problem

7. In graph theory, a _____ in a graph is a sequence of vertices such that from each of its vertices there is an edge to the next vertex in the sequence. The first vertex is called the start vertex and the last vertex is called the end vertex. Both of them are called end or terminal vertices of the _____.

a. Path
b. Class
c. Blinding
d. Deltoid

8. In mathematics, a _____ is a convincing demonstration that some mathematical statement is necessarily true. _____s are obtained from deductive reasoning, rather than from inductive or empirical arguments. That is, a _____ must demonstrate that a statement is true in all cases, without a single exception.

a. Proof
b. Congruent
c. Conchoid
d. Germ

9. In graph theory, a _____ is a digraph with weighted edges. These _____s have become an especially useful concept in analysing the interaction between biology and mathematics. Using _____s of all types; various applications based on the creativity of the mathematician along with their environment can be evaluated in all sorts of manners.

a. Chord
b. Network
c. Colossus
d. Copula

10. _____ is a method of mathematical proof typically used to establish that a given statement is true of all natural numbers. It is done by proving that the first statement in the infinite sequence of statements is true, and then proving that if any one statement in the infinite sequence of statements is true, then so is the next one.

The method can be extended to prove statements about more general well-founded structures, such as trees; this generalization, known as structural induction, is used in mathematical logic and computer science.

a. Ground expression
b. Mathematical Induction
c. Herbrand structure
d. Finitary

11. In mathematics, the _____ is a simple, ancient algorithm for finding all prime numbers up to a specified integer. It works efficiently for the smaller primes . It was created by Eratosthenes, an ancient Greek mathematician.

a. 120-cell
b. 1-center problem
c. 2-3 heap
d. Sieve of Eratosthenes

Chapter 12. Trees

1. In set theory, a _____ is a partially ordered set such that for each t ∈ T, the set {s ∈ T : s < t} is well-ordered by the relation <. For each t ∈ T, the order type of {s ∈ T : s < t} is called the height of t. The height of T itself is the least ordinal greater than the height of each element of T.
    a. Transitive reduction
    b. Definable numbers
    c. Set-theoretic topology
    d. Tree

2. In vascular plants, the _____ is the organ of a plant body that typically lies below the surface of the soil. This is not always the case, however, since a _____ can also be aerial (that is, growing above the ground) or aerating (that is, growing up above the ground or especially above water.) Furthermore, a stem normally occurring below ground is not exceptional either
    a. 2-3 heap
    b. Root
    c. 1-center problem
    d. 120-cell

3. In geometry, a _____ is a special kind of point, usually a corner of a polygon, polyhedron, or higher dimensional polytope. In the geometry of curves a _____ is a point of where the first derivative of curvature is zero. In graph theory, a _____ is the fundamental unit out of which graphs are formed
    a. Crib
    b. Dini
    c. Duality
    d. Vertex

4. A _____ is an area with a high density of trees. There are many definitions of a _____, based on various criteria. These plant communities cover approximately 9.4% of the Earth's surface and function as habitats for organisms, hydrologic flow modulators, and soil conservers, constituting one of the most important aspects of the Earth's biosphere.
    a. 120-cell
    b. 1-center problem
    c. 2-3 heap
    d. Forest

5. _____, in logic and fields that rely on it such as mathematics and philosophy, is a biconditional logical connective between statements. In that it is biconditional, the connective can be likened to the standard material conditional ('if') combined with its reverse ('only if'); hence the name. The result is that the truth of either one of the connected statements requires the truth of the other.

- a. Existential graph
- b. Enumerative definition
- c. Algebraic logic
- d. If and only if

6. In botany, a _____ is an above-ground plant organ specialized for photosynthesis. For this purpose, a _____ is typically flat and thin, to expose the cells containing chloroplast to light over a broad area, and to allow light to penetrate fully into the tissues. Leaves are also the sites in most plants where transpiration and guttation take place.
   - a. 120-cell
   - b. 1-center problem
   - c. 2-3 heap
   - d. Leaf

7. In arithmetic and number theory, the _____ or lowest common multiple or smallest common multiple of two integers a and b is the smallest positive integer that is a multiple of both a and b. Since it is a multiple, it can be divided by a and b without a remainder. If either a or b is 0, so that there is no such positive integer, then lc is defined to be zero.
   - a. Lowest common denominator
   - b. Plus-minus sign
   - c. Least common multiple
   - d. Plus and minus signs

8. In mathematics, a _____ is a convincing demonstration that some mathematical statement is necessarily true. _____s are obtained from deductive reasoning, rather than from inductive or empirical arguments. That is, a _____ must demonstrate that a statement is true in all cases, without a single exception.
   - a. Proof
   - b. Germ
   - c. Congruent
   - d. Conchoid

9. The _____ is a unique, numerical commercial book identifier, based upon the 9-digit Standard Book Numbering code created in the UK by the booksellers and stationers W.H. Smith and others in 1966. The 10-digit _____ format was developed by the International Organization for Standardization and published as an international standard, ISO 2108, in 1970. Currently, the ISO TC 46/SC 9 is responsible for the standard.

a. A posteriori
b. ISBN
c. A Mathematical Theory of Communication
d. A chemical equation

10. The mathematical concept of a _____ expresses the intuitive idea of deterministic dependence between two quantities, one of which is viewed as primary and the other as secondary. A _____ then is a way to associate a unique output for each input of a specified type, for example, a real number or an element of a given set.
   a. Coherent
   b. Grill
   c. Going up
   d. Function

11. In mathematics a _____ is a formal power series whose coefficients encode information about a sequence a_n that is indexed by the natural numbers.

There are various types of _____s, including ordinary _____s, exponential _____s, Lambert series, Bell series, and Dirichlet series; definitions and examples are given below. Every sequence has a _____ of each type.

   a. Combinatorial design
   b. Rule of sum
   c. Restricted sumset
   d. Generating function

12. In the mathematical field of graph theory, a _____ T of a connected, undirected graph G is a tree composed of all the vertices and some of the edges of G. Informally, a _____ of G is a selection of edges of G that form a tree spanning every vertex. That is, every vertex lies in the tree, but no cycles are formed.
   a. Chord
   b. Spanning tree
   c. Germ
   d. Lattice

13. In mathematics, a _____ is a statement that can be proved on the basis of explicitly stated or previously agreed assumptions.

a. Boolean function
b. Theorem
c. Logical value
d. Disjunction introduction

14. In mathematics, computing, linguistics and related subjects, an _____ is a sequence of finite instructions, often used for calculation and data processing. It is formally a type of effective method in which a list of well-defined instructions for completing a task will, when given an initial state, proceed through a well-defined series of successive states, eventually terminating in an end-state. The transition from one state to the next is not necessarily deterministic; some _____s, known as probabilistic _____s, incorporate randomness.

   a. Approximate counting algorithm
   b. In-place algorithm
   c. Out-of-core
   d. Algorithm

15. In general usage, _____ often tends to be used to characterize something with many parts in intricate arrangement. In science there are at this time a number of approaches to characterizing _____, many of which are reflected in Seth Lloyd of M.I.T. writes that he once gave a presentation which set out 32 definitions of _____.

Definitions are often tied to the concept of a 'system' - a set of parts or elements which have relationships among them differentiated from relationships with other elements outside the relational regime.

   a. 2-3 heap
   b. 120-cell
   c. 1-center problem
   d. Complexity

16. In computational complexity theory, the complexity class _____ is a class of problems having two properties:

   - Any given solution to the problem can be verified quickly; the set of problems with this property is called NP.
   - If the problem can be solved quickly, then so can every problem in NP.

Although any given solution to such a problem can be verified quickly, there is no known efficient way to locate a solution in the first place; indeed, the most notable characteristic of _____ problems is that no fast solution to them is known. That is, the time required to solve the problem using any currently known algorithm increases very quickly as the size of the problem grows. As a result, the time required to solve even moderately large versions of many of these problems easily reaches into the billions or trillions of years, using any amount of computing power available today. As a consequence, determining whether or not it is possible to solve these problems quickly is one of the principal unsolved problems in computer science today.

a. Subset sum
b. Quadratic assignment problem
c. NP-complete
d. 3-partition problem

Chapter 13. Depth-First Search and Applications

1. In mathematics, a _____ is a statement that can be proved on the basis of explicitly stated or previously agreed assumptions.
    a. Boolean function
    b. Theorem
    c. Disjunction introduction
    d. Logical value

2. _____ is an algorithm for traversing or searching a tree, tree structure, or graph. One starts at the root and explores as far as possible along each branch before backtracking.

Formally, DFS is an uninformed search that progresses by expanding the first child node of the search tree that appears and thus going deeper and deeper until a goal node is found, or until it hits a node that has no children.

   a. Topological sorting
   b. Depth-limited search
   c. Topological sort
   d. Depth-first search

3. In general usage, _____ often tends to be used to characterize something with many parts in intricate arrangement. In science there are at this time a number of approaches to characterizing _____, many of which are reflected in Seth Lloyd of M.I.T. writes that he once gave a presentation which set out 32 definitions of _____.

Definitions are often tied to the concept of a 'system' - a set of parts or elements which have relationships among them differentiated from relationships with other elements outside the relational regime.

   a. 1-center problem
   b. 2-3 heap
   c. Complexity
   d. 120-cell

4. In graph theory, _____ is a graph search algorithm that begins at the root node and explores all the neighboring nodes. Then for each of those nearest nodes, it explores their unexplored neighbor nodes, and so on, until it finds the goal.

BFS is an uninformed search method that aims to expand and examine all nodes of a graph or combinations of sequence by systematically searching through every solution.

a. Topological sorting
b. Strongly connected component
c. Depth-limited search
d. Breadth-first search

5. In computational complexity theory, the complexity class _____ is a class of problems having two properties:

- Any given solution to the problem can be verified quickly; the set of problems with this property is called NP.
- If the problem can be solved quickly, then so can every problem in NP.

Although any given solution to such a problem can be verified quickly, there is no known efficient way to locate a solution in the first place; indeed, the most notable characteristic of _____ problems is that no fast solution to them is known. That is, the time required to solve the problem using any currently known algorithm increases very quickly as the size of the problem grows. As a result, the time required to solve even moderately large versions of many of these problems easily reaches into the billions or trillions of years, using any amount of computing power available today. As a consequence, determining whether or not it is possible to solve these problems quickly is one of the principal unsolved problems in computer science today.

a. Subset sum
b. 3-partition problem
c. Quadratic assignment problem
d. NP-complete

6. A _____ is a structure built to span a gorge, valley, road, railroad track, river, body of water for the purpose of providing passage over the obstacle. Designs of _____s will vary depending on the function of the _____ and the nature of the terrain where the _____ is to be constructed. Roman _____ of Córdoba, Spain, built in the 1st century BC. Ponte di Pietra in Verona, Italy. A log _____ in the French Alps near Vallorcine. An English 18th century example of a _____ in the Palladian style, with shops on the span: Pulteney _____, Bath A Han Dynasty Chinese miniature model of two residential towers joined by a _____

The first _____s were made by nature -- as simple as a log fallen across a stream.

a. 120-cell
b. Bridge
c. 2-3 heap
d. 1-center problem

7. _____, in logic and fields that rely on it such as mathematics and philosophy, is a biconditional logical connective between statements. In that it is biconditional, the connective can be likened to the standard material conditional ('if') combined with its reverse ('only if'); hence the name. The result is that the truth of either one of the connected statements requires the truth of the other.
   a. If and only if
   b. Enumerative definition
   c. Algebraic logic
   d. Existential graph

8. In mathematics, a _____ is a convincing demonstration that some mathematical statement is necessarily true. _____s are obtained from deductive reasoning, rather than from inductive or empirical arguments. That is, a _____ must demonstrate that a statement is true in all cases, without a single exception.
   a. Conchoid
   b. Congruent
   c. Germ
   d. Proof

9. In geometry, a _____ is a convex regular polyhedron. These are the three-dimensional analogs of the convex regular polygons. There are precisely five such figures.
   a. 1-center problem
   b. 120-cell
   c. 2-3 heap
   d. Platonic solid

Chapter 14. Planar Graphs and Colorings

1. In mathematics, a _____ is, informally, an infinitely vast and infinitely thin sheet. _____s may be thought of as objects in some higher dimensional space, or they may be considered without any outside space, as in the setting of Euclidean geometry
   a. Plane
   b. Bandwidth
   c. Blocking
   d. Group

2. In computational complexity theory, the complexity class _____ is a class of problems having two properties:

   - Any given solution to the problem can be verified quickly; the set of problems with this property is called NP.
   - If the problem can be solved quickly, then so can every problem in NP.

   Although any given solution to such a problem can be verified quickly, there is no known efficient way to locate a solution in the first place; indeed, the most notable characteristic of _____ problems is that no fast solution to them is known. That is, the time required to solve the problem using any currently known algorithm increases very quickly as the size of the problem grows. As a result, the time required to solve even moderately large versions of many of these problems easily reaches into the billions or trillions of years, using any amount of computing power available today. As a consequence, determining whether or not it is possible to solve these problems quickly is one of the principal unsolved problems in computer science today.

   a. Subset sum
   b. Quadratic assignment problem
   c. 3-partition problem
   d. NP-complete

3. In geometry, a _____ is a convex regular polyhedron. These are the three-dimensional analogs of the convex regular polygons. There are precisely five such figures.
   a. 1-center problem
   b. 120-cell
   c. Platonic solid
   d. 2-3 heap

4. In mathematics, a real-valued function f defined on an interval is called _____, concave upwards, concave up or _____ cup, if for any two points x and y in its domain C and any t in [0,1], we have

$$f(tx + (1-t)y) \leq tf(x) + (1-t)f(y).$$

   _____ function on an interval.

In other words, a function is _____ if and only if its epigraph is a _____ set.

Pictorially, a function is called '_____' if the function lies below the straight line segment connecting two points, for any two points in the interval.

A function is called strictly _____ if

$$f(tx + (1-t)y) < tf(x) + (1-t)f(y)$$

for any t in and $x \neq y$.

A function f is said to be concave if − f is _____.

a. Continuous wavelet
b. Convex
c. Continuum
d. Contrapositive

5. A _____ is any polyhedron with twelve faces, but usually a regular _____ is meant: a Platonic solid composed of twelve regular pentagonal faces, with three meeting at each vertex. It has twenty vertices and thirty edges. Its dual polyhedron is the icosahedron.

a. 1-center problem
b. 120-cell
c. 2-3 heap
d. Dodecahedron

6. In geometry, an _____ is any polyhedron having 20 faces, but usually a regular _____ is implied, which has equilateral triangles as faces.

The regular _____ is one of the five Platonic solids. It is a convex regular polyhedron composed of twenty triangular faces, with five meeting at each of the twelve vertices.

a. A Mathematical Theory of Communication
b. A chemical equation
c. A posteriori
d. Icosahedron

7. An _____ is a polyhedron with eight faces. A regular _____ is a Platonic solid composed of eight equilateral triangles, four of which meet at each vertex.

The _____'s symmetry group is O_h, of order 48.

  a. A chemical equation
  b. A Mathematical Theory of Communication
  c. A posteriori
  d. Octahedron

8. A _____ is often defined as a geometric object with flat faces and straight edges .

This definition of a _____ is not very precise, and to a modern mathematician is quite unsatisfactory. Grünbaum observed that:

The Original Sin in the theory of polyhedra goes back to Euclid, and through Kepler, Poinsot, Cauchy and many others ...

  a. 120-cell
  b. 1-center problem
  c. 2-3 heap
  d. Polyhedron

9. In mathematics, a _____ is a convincing demonstration that some mathematical statement is necessarily true. _____s are obtained from deductive reasoning, rather than from inductive or empirical arguments. That is, a _____ must demonstrate that a statement is true in all cases, without a single exception.
  a. Conchoid
  b. Germ
  c. Congruent
  d. Proof

10. A _____ is a polyhedron composed of four triangular faces, three of which meet at each vertex. A regular _____ is one in which the four triangles are regular, or 'equilateral', and is one of the Platonic solids.

The _____ is one kind of pyramid, which is a polyhedron with a flat polygon base and triangular faces connecting the base to a common point.

Chapter 14. Planar Graphs and Colorings

a. 120-cell
b. 2-3 heap
c. 1-center problem
d. Tetrahedron

11. In the mathematical field of topology, a homeomorphism or topological isomorphism = similar and μορφÎ® = shape = form) is a bicontinuous function between two topological spaces. Homeomorphisms are the isomorphisms in the category of topological spaces -- that is, they are the mappings which preserve all the topological properties of a given space. Two spaces with a homeomorphism between them are called _____, and from a topological viewpoint they are the same.
    a. 2-3 heap
    b. 120-cell
    c. 1-center problem
    d. Homeomorphic

12. In mathematics, a _____ is a statement that can be proved on the basis of explicitly stated or previously agreed assumptions.
    a. Theorem
    b. Disjunction introduction
    c. Boolean function
    d. Logical value

13. In mathematics, the _____ is a direct product of sets. The _____ is named after René Descartes, whose formulation of analytic geometry gave rise to this concept.

Specifically, the _____ of two sets X and Y, denoted X × Y, is the set of all possible ordered pairs whose first component is a member of X and whose second component is a member of Y:

$$X \times Y = \{(x,y) | x \in X \text{ and } y \in Y\}.$$

For example, the _____ of the 13-element set of standard playing card ranks {Ace, King, Queen, Jack, 10, 9, 8, 7, 6, 5, 4, 3, 2} and the four-element set of card suits {â™ , â™¥, â™¦, â™£} is the 52-element set of all possible playing cards ,, ...,,, ...,}.

a. Set of all sets
b. Cartesian product
c. Choice function
d. Disjoint sets

Chapter 14. Planar Graphs and Colorings

14. In the mathematical area of order theory, every partially ordered set P gives rise to a _____ partially ordered set which is often denoted by P^{op} or P^d. This _____ order P^{op} is defined to be the set with the inverse order. It is easy to see that this construction, which can be depicted by flipping the Hasse diagram for P upside down, will indeed yield a partially ordered set.
    a. Contraction mapping
    b. Dual
    c. Context-sensitive language
    d. Christofides heuristics

15. In mathematics, a _____ of a given planar graph G is a graph which has a vertex for each plane region of G, and an edge for each edge in G joining two neighboring regions, for a certain embedding of G. The term 'dual' is used because this property is symmetric, meaning that if H is a dual of G, then G is a dual of H. The same notation of duality may also be used for more general embeddings of graphs on manifolds.
    a. Covering code
    b. Graph theory
    c. McCarthy 91 function
    d. Dual graph

Chapter 15. The Max Flow-Min Cut Theorem

1. In mathematics, the _____ is a simple, ancient algorithm for finding all prime numbers up to a specified integer. It works efficiently for the smaller primes. It was created by Eratosthenes, an ancient Greek mathematician.
   a. 1-center problem
   b. 2-3 heap
   c. 120-cell
   d. Sieve of Eratosthenes

2. In graph theory, a _____ is a digraph with weighted edges. These _____s have become an especially useful concept in analysing the interaction between biology and mathematics. Using _____s of all types; various applications based on the creativity of the mathematician along with their environment can be evaluated in all sorts of manners.
   a. Copula
   b. Colossus
   c. Chord
   d. Network

3. In plumbing, a _____ or basin is a bowl-shaped fixture that is used for washing hands or small objects such as food, dishes, nylons, socks or underwear. In American plumbing parlance, a bathroom _____ is known as a lavatory.

   _____s generally have taps that supply hot and cold water and may include a spray feature to be used for faster rinsing.

   a. 1-center problem
   b. 2-3 heap
   c. Sink
   d. 120-cell

4. In mathematics, a _____ is a statement that can be proved on the basis of explicitly stated or previously agreed assumptions.
   a. Disjunction introduction
   b. Theorem
   c. Boolean function
   d. Logical value

5. _____ is the mathematical operation of scaling one number by another. It is one of the four basic operations in elementary arithmetic.

_____ is defined for whole numbers in terms of repeated addition; for example, 4 multiplied by 3 can be calculated by adding 3 copies of 4 together:

$$4 + 4 + 4 = 12.$$

_____ of rational numbers and real numbers is defined by systematic generalization of this basic idea.

a. Least common multiple
b. Highest common factor
c. Multiplication
d. The number 0 is even.

6. _____ is a systematic method for multiplying two numbers that does not require the multiplication table, only the ability to multiply and divide by 2, and to add. Also known as Egyptian multiplication and Peasant multiplication, it decomposes one of the multiplicands into a sum of powers of two and creates a table of doublings of the second multiplicand. This method may be called mediation and duplation, where mediation means halving one number and duplation means doubling the other number.
   a. A chemical equation
   b. A Mathematical Theory of Communication
   c. A posteriori
   d. Ancient Egyptian multiplication

7. In mathematics, a measure is said to be _____ if every locally measurable set is also measurable.
   a. Transverse measure
   b. Green measure
   c. Saturated
   d. Pushforward measure

8. In number theory, a _____ of a positive integer n is a way of writing n as a sum of positive integers. Two sums which only differ in the order of their summands are considered to be the same _____; if order matters then the sum becomes a composition. A summand in a _____ is also called a part.
   a. Congruent
   b. Derivative algebra
   c. Partition
   d. Distribution

9. In the mathematical field of graph theory, a _____ is a path in an undirected graph which visits each vertex exactly once. A Hamiltonian cycle is a cycle in an undirected graph which visits each vertex exactly once and also returns to the starting vertex. Determining whether such paths and cycles exist in graphs is the _____ problem which is NP-complete.
   a. Centrality
   b. Complex network
   c. Graceful labeling
   d. Hamiltonian path

10. _____ was a mathematician of great scope and depth.

He was the son of the famous economist Carl Menger.

He worked in mathematics on algebras, curve and dimension theory, and geometries.

   a. Gustave Bertrand
   b. Karl Menger
   c. Solomon Lefschetz
   d. Frederick William Winterbotham

11. In graph theory, a _____ in a graph is a sequence of vertices such that from each of its vertices there is an edge to the next vertex in the sequence. The first vertex is called the start vertex and the last vertex is called the end vertex. Both of them are called end or terminal vertices of the _____.
   a. Deltoid
   b. Class
   c. Blinding
   d. Path

12. _____ or set diagrams are diagrams that show all hypothetically possible logical relations between a finite collection of sets. _____ were invented around 1880 by John Venn. They are used in many fields, including set theory, probability, logic, statistics, and computer science.
   a. Venn diagrams
   b. 1-center problem
   c. 2-3 heap
   d. 120-cell

13. A _____ is a 2D geometric symbolic representation of information according to some visualization technique. Sometimes, the technique uses a 3D visualization which is then projected onto the 2D surface. The word graph is sometimes used as a synonym for _____.

a. Diagram
b. 1-center problem
c. 2-3 heap
d. 120-cell

14. In the mathematical discipline of graph theory a _____ or edge independent set in a graph is a set of edges without common vertices. It may also be an entire graph consisting of edges without common vertices.

Given a graph G =, a _____ M in G is a set of pairwise non-adjacent edges; that is, no two edges share a common vertex.

a. Cut vertex
b. Route inspection problem
c. Matching
d. Road coloring theorem

15. In mathematics, in the realm of group theory, a group is said to be _____ if it equals its own commutator subgroup if the group has no nontrivial abelian quotients.

The smallest _____ group is the alternating group A_5. More generally, any non-abelian simple group is _____ since the commutator subgroup is a normal subgroup with abelian quotient.

a. Quaternion group
b. Group of Lie type
c. Free product
d. Perfect

16. In geometry, a _____ is a special kind of point, usually a corner of a polygon, polyhedron, or higher dimensional polytope. In the geometry of curves a _____ is a point of where the first derivative of curvature is zero. In graph theory, a _____ is the fundamental unit out of which graphs are formed
a. Dini
b. Crib
c. Duality
d. Vertex

17. In mathematics, a _____ is a convincing demonstration that some mathematical statement is necessarily true. _____s are obtained from deductive reasoning, rather than from inductive or empirical arguments. That is, a _____ must demonstrate that a statement is true in all cases, without a single exception.
   a. Germ
   b. Conchoid
   c. Proof
   d. Congruent

18. The mathematical concept of a _____ expresses the intuitive idea of deterministic dependence between two quantities, one of which is viewed as primary and the other as secondary. A _____ then is a way to associate a unique output for each input of a specified type, for example, a real number or an element of a given set.
   a. Coherent
   b. Grill
   c. Going up
   d. Function

Chapter 1
1. d 2. a 3. d 4. d 5. b 6. d 7. d 8. d 9. c 10. a
11. a 12. b 13. a 14. b 15. a 16. d 17. d 18. a 19. b 20. b
21. b 22. d 23. d 24. b 25. a 26. c 27. d 28. d 29. a

Chapter 2
1. d 2. a 3. b 4. d 5. c 6. d 7. d 8. a 9. d 10. b
11. d 12. b 13. b 14. a 15. d 16. a 17. b 18. d 19. d 20. a
21. d 22. a 23. d 24. b 25. c 26. c 27. d 28. d 29. d 30. a
31. b 32. a 33. d 34. d 35. a 36. d 37. d 38. a 39. b 40. b

Chapter 3
1. d 2. c 3. c 4. d 5. a 6. d 7. b 8. d 9. d 10. d
11. d 12. b 13. c 14. b 15. b 16. d 17. c 18. d 19. d 20. b
21. d 22. d 23. d 24. d 25. d

Chapter 4
1. b 2. a 3. a 4. b 5. d 6. c 7. a 8. a 9. b 10. d
11. a 12. d 13. a 14. a 15. b 16. a 17. c 18. d 19. d 20. d
21. d 22. d 23. a 24. a 25. d 26. a 27. b 28. b 29. a 30. a
31. c 32. c 33. c 34. d 35. d 36. d 37. b 38. d 39. d 40. a
41. d 42. d 43. d 44. c 45. a 46. d 47. c 48. d 49. c 50. d
51. c 52. b

Chapter 5
1. d 2. a 3. b 4. d 5. d 6. d 7. d 8. a 9. a 10. d
11. d 12. d 13. d 14. a 15. c 16. c 17. a 18. d 19. d 20. a
21. d 22. d 23. d 24. a 25. d 26. d 27. c

Chapter 6
1. d 2. b 3. d 4. a 5. c 6. b 7. c

Chapter 7
1. c 2. a 3. d 4. d 5. b 6. d 7. d 8. d 9. a 10. d

Chapter 8
1. d 2. d 3. d 4. d 5. b 6. d 7. d 8. b 9. b 10. b
11. c 12. a 13. d 14. b 15. d 16. b 17. b 18. b 19. d 20. d
21. a 22. b 23. b 24. d 25. d 26. b 27. a 28. c 29. d 30. d
31. c

Chapter 9
1. c 2. d 3. b 4. d 5. d 6. d 7. d 8. d 9. c 10. d
11. d 12. c 13. c 14. d 15. a 16. d 17. d

ANSWER KEY

Chapter 10
1. d　2. d　3. b　4. a　5. a　6. a　7. d　8. d　9. a　10. d
11. d　12. d　13. d　14. a　15. d　16. d　17. d　18. a　19. a　20. a
21. b　22. a　23. d　24. c

Chapter 11
1. d　2. d　3. d　4. a　5. a　6. b　7. a　8. a　9. b　10. b
11. d

Chapter 12
1. d　2. b　3. d　4. d　5. d　6. d　7. c　8. a　9. b　10. d
11. d　12. b　13. b　14. d　15. d　16. c

Chapter 13
1. b　2. d　3. c　4. d　5. d　6. b　7. a　8. d　9. d

Chapter 14
1. a　2. d　3. c　4. b　5. d　6. d　7. d　8. d　9. d　10. d
11. d　12. a　13. b　14. b　15. d

Chapter 15
1. d　2. d　3. c　4. b　5. c　6. d　7. c　8. c　9. d　10. b
11. d　12. a　13. a　14. c　15. d　16. d　17. c　18. d

www.ingramcontent.com/pod-product-compliance
Lightning Source LLC
Chambersburg PA
CBHW082051230426
43670CB00016B/2856